Hinduism

Beliefs and Practices

The Sussex Library of Religious Beliefs and Practices

Published

Sikhism
W. Owen Cole and Piara Singh Sambhi

Hinduism
Jeaneane Fowler

The Jews
Alan Unterman

Forthcoming

Buddhism	*Christianity*		*The Ancient Egyptians*	
Humanism	*Islam*	*Jainism*	*Zen*	*Zoroastrianism*

This series is intended for students of religion, social sciences and history, and for the interested layperson. It is concerned with the beliefs and practices of religions in their social, cultural and historical setting.

Other religious titles of interest

Confucianism and Christianity: A Comparative Study of Jen and Agape
Xinzhong Yao

The Bible as Theatre
Theatre and Holy Script (anthology of essays)
Shimon Levy

Jainism: The World of Conquerors (2 volumes)
Natubhai Shah

World Religions: An Introduction for Students
Jeaneane Fowler (editor), Merv Fowler, David Norcliffe, Diane Watkins, Nora Hill

The Supreme Doctrine: Psychological Studies in Zen Thought
Hubert Benoit, with Forewords by Aldous Huxley and Tim Barrett

Glimpses of the Divine: A Spiritual Anthology for Use on Every Day of the Year
Cyril Bulley

Hinduism

Beliefs and Practices

JEANEANE FOWLER

sussex
ACADEMIC
PRESS

Copyright © Jeaneane Fowler 1997

The right of Jeaneane Fowler to be identified as author of this work has been asserted in accordance with the Copyright, Designs and Patents Act 1988.

First published 1997 in Great Britain by
SUSSEX ACADEMIC PRESS
18 Chichester Place
Brighton BN2 1FF

and in the United States of America by
SUSSEX ACADEMIC PRESS
c/o International Specialized Book Services, Inc.
5804 N.E. Hassalo St.
Portland, Oregon 97213-3644

British Library Cataloguing in Publication Data

A CIP catalogue record for this book is available from the British Library.

ISBN 1–898723 60 5 (paperback)

Front cover picture: Rama, Sita and Laksman crossing the river Ganges at the beginning of their fourteen years of exile. Detail from a cloth print, India.

Printed and bound by Biddles Ltd, King's Lynn and Guildford
This book is printed on acid free paper

Contents

Foreword

Dr Jeaneane Fowler is a highly successful teacher who generates great enthusiasm in her students, an increasing number of whom go on to read for higher degrees including PhDs. Her own interest is in eastern philosophies generally and this means that she is able to place Hinduism, as the current example, in a wider context than that of being only the dominant Indian expression of religion.

There has often been a tendency among western writers to stress the philosophy but to neglect the expression of Hinduism which is experienced in everyday life in the villages, and often in city life too, and the seemingly endless round of festivals. Dr Fowler does not fall into this trap. Neither does she suffer from the desire, sometimes demonstrated by Hindu authors, to present the religion as simple, straightforward and rather bland. Instead, she presents the religion like a *thali*, in which different flavours interact to produce a single fascinating dish. In seeking to present the unity which is Hinduism, the author does not lose the rich diversity of the *thali*, which is also Hinduism.

Students and others will be enriched as they encounter Hinduism in Dr Fowler's company.

Dr W. Owen Cole
Chichester Institute of Higher Education
West Sussex

Preface and Acknowledgements

In recent times interest in religions of the East has grown enormously, not only in the academic field in terms of the kinds of subjects which students wish to study, but also in society at large. In particular, religions like Hinduism and Buddhism have given the Western world much to think about, with doctrines such as reincarnation, non-violence and the importance of meditation, for example. The word *karma* – unknown to many people a half century ago – has become almost a household term. It is an interest which has to some extent arisen out of a Western world which has lost touch with itself and which is searching for something which it knows not, but believes the East has found! This has led to rather stereotyped visions of Eastern religions, and this book is designed as the kind of introduction to the religion of Hinduism which will lead the reader step-by-step to a more valid understanding of the phenomenon of Hinduism. Yet much of that discovery will elicit the fact that there really is no *one* phenomenon which could be called Hinduism and that Hinduism is a rich variety of beliefs and practices.

The book is also designed for the student who is new to Hinduism but who has sufficient interest in it to embark on a course of study in the subject. The material presented in the book therefore assumes no prior knowledge but seeks to guide the student through some of the major aspects of the religion so that he or she is equipped with essential information for further study. In many ways, then, the book is a *true* introduction – the meeting of a subject for the first time.

In terms of content, the material is informed by two purposes. The first is to present a picture of the variety of beliefs and practices which make up *living* Hinduism; that is to say, what it means to be a Hindu in the world of today. The older approaches of treating the subject entirely historically will not be found here, for essentially it is hoped that after reading this book there would be enough knowledge about Hinduism today to enter into *dialogue* with any Hindu: it is thus meant as a starting point for inter-cultural or inter-faith communion. But there are historical aspects which inform today's practices, and part of the purpose of this book will be to outline such influences.

I owe a considerable debt to the many students who have studied with me and who have been co-explorers with me in the field of Hinduism. It is they who have indicated the need for such a book and whose enthusiasm for Hinduism has given me some of the most rewarding years of my life. Anthony Grahame at Sussex Academic Press has always been available personally for advice at every stage of this book and has contributed so much to making it an enjoyable experience to write as well as being totally supportive during difficult times. While every effort has been made on my part to ensure that this work is free from error, any mistakes which remain are entirely my own. Finally I owe a very special acknowledgement to my colleague and husband Merv who shares my enthusiasm for Eastern religions and the enjoyable task of imparting it to students. It is to you Merv that, once again, I dedicate a book with all my love and gratitude.

University of Wales College, Newport
October 1996

I HAVE MET thee where the night touches the edge of the day; where the light startles the darkness into dawn, and the waves carry the kiss of the one shore to the other.

From the heart of the fathomless blue comes one golden call, and across the dusk of tears I try to gaze at thy face and know not for certain if thou art seen.

Rabindranath Tagore

Introduction

Knowledge and Acquaintance

The religion which we term Hinduism is mainly an Indian phenomenon, but Hindus can also be found throughout Asia, in Africa, the West Indies and Indonesia as well as in a number of countries in which they have been immigrants. It is something of a unique religion because it has no founder and so no point in time when it could be said to have begun, and none of the core doctrines which are so often associated with a founder. While it would be true to say that many religions lack uniformity, Hinduism, in particular, is characterized by immense diversity. It is precisely this lack of uniformity which makes it such an attractive religion to study, for Hinduism reflects the multiplicity of shades of human aspirations in the religious and spiritual dimensions of existence. It is almost impossible to study Hinduism without coming across religious perspectives which make sense in terms of one's own perspectives of religion, even if they are atheist, for Hinduism caters for all levels of consciousness and personal stages on the evolutionary path through life.

Then, too, Hinduism has been fed by very different cultural traditions, from its prehistoric beginnings so far back in time, to modern times in which local custom may even dictate the rise of a new deity. From the earliest times a predominantly village culture in a vast country meant that different religious ideas obtained and existed side by side, sometimes with minor variations but often with marked contrasts. This is another dimension in which Hinduism is unique, for an attitude which accommodates religious and cultural perspectives other than one's own, seems to be part of the Indian psyche. This is another reason why the religion is characterized by such a rich variety of ideas and practices resulting in what appears as a multiplicity of religions under that one term *Hinduism*. So Hinduism, as probably the oldest religion in the world, has added many strands to its overall character in thousands of years. Additionally, outside influences have been accommodated also: the Aryan migrations in the second century BCE left an indelible socio-religious character on what developed into the Hindu religion as we know it today. But indigenous beliefs and practices survived and, though they were not evident in the Aryan scriptures, surfaced in one way or another as time went by. Indeed Hinduism could never be neatly slotted into any particular belief system – monism, theism, monotheism, polytheism, pantheism, panentheism – for all these systems are reflected in its many facets.

The student of Hinduism has a fascinating journey of exploration ahead but it is a journey which requires some preparation. Westerners are so accustomed to living life according to linear beliefs and patterns of existence: we have to have a beginning, middle and end of things or method, result and conclusion, for the comfort of our own minds, and many students will be aware of their tutors' requests for work which has an introduction, main body of material and conclusion. Our lives, too, are viewed in the linear concept of one birth, life and death. But Hinduism is not like this for it has little interest in, for example, the linear nature of history or a linear pattern of life. What Hinduism has instead is a *cyclical* perspective of life, even of the cosmos itself. This means that time is viewed differently and there is a cosmic perspective to it which has pervaded Hinduism from the time of the Aryans onwards: death is not the end of the line but the door to the next cycle, to birth – and this is true of the universe itself as much as the human being. Westerners are less aware of the cyclical patterns in the rhythms of nature but the student of Hinduism would be advised to travel with this somewhat different perspective. Importantly, too, the student needs to travel with an open mind, exploring the dimensions of Hinduism like completing a jigsaw puzzle and not prejudging the effect until the last piece is in place. And the best way to travel is without baggage for it leaves one free and unhindered: this is no less the case with the mind which does well when it remains uncluttered by prejudice or biased conceptions. It is hoped, too, that some students will have sufficient interest to journey further than this book can take them.

The book is divided into two parts, *The Hindu Way of Life* and *History and Tradition*. The former deals with *living* Hinduism and analyses the basic ideas and practices which inform Hinduism today. This first part seeks to enable the reader to have a sufficient understanding of what it is to be a Hindu to be able to enter into dialogue with people from the Hindu faith – the means by which the best understanding of the religion can be gained. Because *Part One* stands as a gentle introduction to Hinduism it is not replete with burdensome references and notes on the text. *Part Two, History and Tradition* seeks to show how present beliefs and practices have been informed by past traditions and the ways in which those beliefs and practices have been accommodated in Hinduism today. The term *History* is not a good one for Indians generally are not particularly interested in such a linear concept, but it serves to illustrate that this section is delving into past ideas. Essentially it is a section more interested in concepts than historical portrayal. There is some difference in the style of *Part Two* since the reader who has explored *Part One* should be ready for a second level of exploration. Here, then, the material is dealt with in slightly more depth, and more detailed annotation of the text is included.

Sanskrit terms have been retained throughout as much as possible so that the reader can become accustomed to them. The terms have not been Anglicized too much (unless they are well-known words such as *karma*). A glossary of Sanskrit terms is included at the end of the book and the reader is advised to study these from time to time to help with pronunciation of the words as much as with meaning. Diacritical marks have not been included in the text and the glossary, therefore, will be a valuable tool. A select bibliography is also included.

Finally, there are many concepts which are not dealt with in the context of this book, which has kept somewhat strictly to its remit of beliefs and practices. But Hinduism has such a broad tapestry of ideas and practices that it would be an impossible task to encompass them all. Hinduism is a religion which has aspects to suit all levels of consciousness and accepts the evolutionary nature of the self. Whatever is expolored in Hinduism can always be re-explored from the perspective of a *higher* level of consciousness when different perspectives will emerge. It is a religion of all possibilities.

Part One

The Hindu Way of Life

1

Fundamental Beliefs

The meaning of the term Hinduism

The term *Hinduism* is misleading for it suggests a unified system of beliefs and ideas, which is certainly not the case. It was, in fact, an 'ism' given by nineteenth century English people to the multiplicity of beliefs which we today know as Hinduism. It is not a term 'Hindus' themselves would normally use, and the term 'Hindu' itself originated as a geographical one for those who lived beyond the river (S)indu. Hinduism is much too broad a phenomenon to be confined to the usual definitions of religion. It represents a whole spectrum of beliefs and practices which on the one hand contains veneration of trees and stones and the like, and on the other very profound, abstract, metaphysical speculations. Similarly, there are no criteria for establishing *who* is a Hindu because no two Hindus will necessarily think alike; there are no uniformly accepted beliefs, sacraments, rituals and practices to make this possible. So from the outset it can be seen that there is a considerable contrast between Hinduism and many other religions. Additionally, there is no religious founder in Hinduism: rather, Hinduism has evolved from a multiplicity of ideas which have largely never been discarded but have been retained alongside each other. It would, therefore, be more correct to speak of *Hinduisms* than of Hinduism in the singular.

In the 5000 and more years of the history of Hinduism few aspects have been lost: new ideas have always been accommodated alongside the old ones. This is partly why, when visiting a Hindu temple, we are likely to see pictures of Jesus of Nazareth, Guru Nanak or the Buddha, alongside those of Hindu deities. At the philosophical level, it is impossible to categorize Hinduism into any *particular* belief system such as monotheistic, pantheistic, panentheistiic, theistic, monistic and so on. Hinduism is *all* of these.

It is this kind of accommodation of a multiplicity of ideas which is at the heart of Hinduism and such a tolerance of ideas comes about because of a deep belief in the differences in the levels of consciousness of individuals. No two human beings are the same, and the Hindu would regard it as rather illogical, therefore, to expect two people to have the same views of God, the same level of understanding, the same beliefs, or the same needs and practices. Because each individual is an evolving, changing, entity his or her individual level of consciousness will necessitate an individual approach to God, different from the approach of another. The nature of the Hindu deity is *absolute*; that is to say it has all the possible qualities of the cosmos and can be perceived from any angle. And it depends on one's level of consciousness how one is *able* to perceive that divine entity. To say that everyone must have the same view is nonsensical to the Hindu.

Hinduism has little interest in history, historical dates and a linear approach to its development. More important is tradition – the past being manifest in the present. Countries and governments and, indeed, civilizations have come and gone, while India, the home of most Hindus, has remained very much the same. Many of the scenes witnessed today in India are remarkably similar to those of 4000 years ago! It is tradition which has made this possible. Tradition for the Hindu is *religious* tradition since religion and culture are one and the same thing, with no division between the religious and the secular. Indeed, since *religion* is not an independent phenomenon in Hinduism there is, in fact, no term for it; instead, emotive terms like *bhakti* 'devotion' or *dharma* 'what is right' and *yoga* 'discipline' depict essential aspects of religion, as well as practical aspects like *varnasramadharma*, which we shall examine below. A word like *sadhana*, which has no direct translation in English, depicts Hindu religion rather well. Its basic root *sadha* has many meanings – 'to reach one's goal', 'to subdue', 'to gain power over', 'to fulfil', 'to accomplish an aim' – and involves the idea of an individual reaching the fullest spiritual potential and perfection.[1] In reaching spiritual perfection, however, there is no claim that any one way or interpretation is correct.

The Hindu concept of God

Although many people associate Hinduism with a multiplicity of Gods, in fact there is only one supreme Absolute, so *absolute* that we could not even use the term *God* to depict it. This Absolute is called Brahman and everything in life, whether living or not comes from Brahman. Every creature, every plant, every individual, every stone, every tree – everything in existence – has its source as Brahman. This means that Brahman is in all things and each thing is a part of Brahman; this is called *pantheism* (*pan* 'all', *theism* 'of God'). Because Brahman is in all things, all things can be regarded as sacred in their essence and Hindus call this essence *atman*. To keep the idea of Brahman as Absolute, Brahman is an *It*. This is why we cannot call Brahman *God*, because if we did, we would be making God male rather than female. God would then be describable and this would limit the concept of an Absolute. Brahman, then, cannot be described by humankind in any way: it is totally beyond anything that humankind can conceive of and is *nirakara* 'without form'. However, because Brahman is in all things in the cosmos it can be *manifest* in a myriad of forms and it is in this way that Brahman can also be seen in the many Gods and Goddesses of Hinduism as *sakara* 'with form'.

Although there are many manifestations of Brahman in the forms of deities each deity is really an aspect of Brahman or, ultimately, Brahman itself. And since Brahman is in all things then there is no reason why Brahman cannot be manifest in feminine forms as well as masculine ones. The relationship between the many manifest deities and the Unmanifest Brahman is rather like that between the sun and its rays. We cannot experience the sun itself but we can experience its rays and the qualities which those rays have. And although the sun's rays are many, ultimately, there is only one source, one sun. So the Gods and Goddesses of Hinduism amount to thousands, all representing the many aspects of Brahman. The Hindu deities will be examined in more detail below, but here three major deities need to be mentioned: Visnu, Siva and the Mother Goddess. Worshippers of Visnu are called Vaisnavites. Visnu represents Brahman as the sustainer of the universe. He is an important deity because whenever the world becomes too evil Visnu is said to incarnate himself on earth to restore good. Two of the most important incarnations of Visnu on earth are in his form as Ram and in his form as Krisna: many Vaisnavites in particular prefer to worship Brahman in such incarnate form rather than Visnu.

The other major deity is Siva who represents the force of dissolution in the universe. Those who worship Siva are known as Saivites. Siva represents the more awe-inspiring aspects of Brahman, those more closely associated with death and destruction, yet Siva balances all the opposites in life, good and bad, light and dark, evolution and devolution,

life and death and so on. He is a more difficult deity to understand. The
Mother Goddess takes many forms. She is known as the *sakti* energy
in life. In fact, each male deity like Visnu or Siva has its *sakti* energy,
its female energy which is itself a deity. So the female *sakti* of Visnu is
the Goddess Laksmi, the Goddess responsible for good fortune, while
the *sakti* energy of Siva takes many forms: these can be violent, like
the Goddesses Durga and Kali, or mild like Uma and Parvati. Siva will
always have opposites in his own form and therefore in his female *sakti*
forms too.

Samsara: the cycle of reincarnation

Hinduism accepts the concept of reincarnation, the idea that at the end
of each life, the individual is born again in another existence in order
to carry on his or her evolutionary path. Hindus see all life as cyclical,
evident in the cycles of the planets, of trees and plants, of nature, of
the universe and of humankind too. Apart from the physical body and
the breath which makes us live, Hindus see the individual as composed
of two elements. One is the personality self, called the *jivatman* and the
other is the part of the individual which is Brahman and which is called
atman. The *jivatman* is our personality; it is constantly changing and is the
sum total of all our experiences in life, all our desires and aversions and all
our conscious and subconscious characteristics. The *atman*, on the other
hand, is the part of us which is Brahman, which cannot change, which
is permanent, and which, like Brahman, is Absolute. The *atman* does not
reincarnate at all; it is simple *there* in everything which is manifest in the
world. It is the *jivatman* which is subject to reincarnation and the next
reincarnation of a *jivatman* will depend entirely on the personality of an
individual in the present existence. The *Brhadaranyaka Upanisad* describes
this very well: *According to*

> *a person*
> An individual creates for himself his next life as a result of his desires,
> hopes, aspirations, failures, disappointments, achievements and actions
> performed during this life of his. Just as a caterpillar, before it leaves
> one leaf, makes sure that his front feet have been firmly fixed on the
> next leaf of the branch of a tree, a *jivatman* creates its next life before
> it departs from the present one.[2]

What determines the state of the individual in the next existence, is
karma.

Karma: the law of cause and effect

Karma means 'act', 'action' or 'activity' and refers, not only to actions undertaken by the body, but also to those undertaken by the mind. *Karma* is actually action *and reaction* for Hindus believe that all actions produce results and it is this theory that is behind the concept of *samsara*. As we know from life itself, not all actions produce immediate results, particularly those actions of the mind, so it may be a very long time before the results of certain actions, whether physical or mental, come to fruition. This means that results of actions may come about in later existences. It is the *jivatman*, the personality with its many positive and negative likes and dislikes and positive and negative actions, which causes *karma*. Every time we do something or think something, we create a cause and having created a cause we must have an effect, a result.

So each individual goes through life creating the kinds of results which will be stored up to form his or her *jivatman* in the next existence. Each person chooses how to act or think, so each person's *karma* is his or her own and equally so the results of those choices belong to that person. So if choices are good, then results in the next life will be good, but if choices are bad then the just rewards of such will be reaped also in subsequent lives. If actions are very bad then a person may actually *devolve* and degenerate into a lower life form as an animal. Westerners sometimes see the operation of *karma* as fatalistic, but it is far from this, since, while an individual can do nothing about the *karma* he or she must reap, all of an individual's future lives are affected by present actions, thoughts and words: we shape our own future. And while it is also suggested by some that the *status quo* in India is maintained with regard to poverty, there are many Hindus who would counter-claim that reponsibility and care for the poor is one of the means by which good *karma* can be promoted.

Dharma: what is right

In order to achieve good *karma* it is important to live life according to *dharma*, what is right. This involves doing what is right for the individual, the family, the class or caste and also for the universe itself. *Dharma* is like a cosmic norm and if one goes against the cosmic norm or the norm for the individual or class, then bad *karma* can result. But *dharma* also affects the future, for each individual has his or her own *dharmic* path dependent on the *karma* which has been accumulated. So one's *dharmic* path in the next life is the one necessary to bring to fruition all the results of past *karma* and is thus right for the individual, even though it may be a difficult path.

Moksa: liberation from *samsara*

The ultimate aim of every Hindu is that one day the endless cycle of *samsara* will be over and there will be no necessity to be reincarnated. This can only happen when there is no *karma* to cause an individual to be reincarnated because there is no egoistic self, no 'I' to reap any results. This is *moksa*, liberation from the cycle of *samsara*. It is thus achieved when the *jivatman* loses its good and bad *karma* and has no *karma* at all. To achieve this Hindus have many paths, it is not something which can be achieved in only one way. But when a person realizes *moksa*, the *atman* – the part of the individual which is Brahman – merges with Brahman like the river merges into the sea. The *jivatman* is gone and only pure *atman*, which is Brahman, remains.

2

Hindu Scriptures

Sruti and smrti literature

There are two kinds of sacred writings in Hinduism, *sruti* and *smrti*. *Sruti* literature is the oldest and more sacred. For a long time it was handed down orally before being committed to writing. The spoken word in religious practice has always been important in Hinduism: priests may recite from memory, or occasionally read from the scriptures, but to *hear* scripture is itself an act of devotion. *Sruti* means 'heard', 'perceived', 'understood', or 'cognized' and refers to the habit of the ancient seers of Hinduism going off to live in the forests alone, where they became so holy and so evolved in consciousness that they could 'hear' or 'cognize' the truths of the universe. The teachings they left for the Hindus who came after them through the centuries are believed to be universal laws, unchangeable and eternal. *Sruti* literature is divided into two main parts, the *Vedas* and the *Upanisads*. The word *veda* means 'knowledge' while the word *upanisad* means 'sitting down near to', probably referring to the disciples of the seers, who sat down in the forest at the feet of their teachers, or *gurus*, to learn about these truths of the universe. There are four *Vedas*: the *Rg Veda* or 'Royal Knowledge', the *Sama Veda* 'Knowledge of Chants', *Yajur Veda* 'Knowledge of Sacrificial Ritual' and *Atharva Veda* 'Knowledge of Incantations'. There are many more *upanisads*, but scholars generally agree that about thirteen of these are the most important.

Smrti literature is not so sacred but is just as important. It is *smrti* literature which is popular with most Hindus today. *Smrti* means 'memory', 'remembered', and this literature is generally much easier to understand because it points to the truths of the universe through the medium of symbolism and mythology, and through some of the most beautiful and exciting stories in the history of religion. So popular is some of this *smrti* literature that in recent years when some of it has been made into serials for television, the entire inhabitants of a village, young, old, men and women, would gather round one television set to watch as many as 96 weekly episodes.

The *Mahabharat*

Though there are many writings within the *smrti* literature, three stand out as being very famous. These are the *Ramayan*, the *Mahabharat*, and the *Bhagavad Gita*. The *Mahabharat* is the world's longest poem and dates back to about the ninth century BCE. *Mahabharat* means 'The great story of the Bharatas' and it tells the story of a tremendous struggle for power between two royal families, the Pandavas and the Kauravas. The King, Bharata (which is the old name for India), had two sons, Pandu and Dhritarasta. Pandu had five sons who were very noble and good, representing *dharma* in life, while Dhritarasta had a hundred sons who were generally evil and who represented *adharma* in life. The story of the power struggle between these two parties, the five Pandavas and the hundred Kauravas, forms the story of the *Mahabharat* and into this story are interwoven all kinds of episodes of love, war, intrigue, relationships and all the countless situations which make up life. Like much *smrti* literature, the stories can be told to children, to adults, to intellectuals or to the simple; it will depend on the individual level of consciousness as to what will be gleaned from the narrative. The attentive listener, however, will discern much moral, social, political and religious teaching in these stories.

The *Bhagavad Gita*

The *Bhagavad Gita*, 'Song of the Adorable One', is perhaps the most well-known Hindu scripture. It is actually the sixth part of the *Mahabharat* but is usually referred to separately. It was probably written in about the second century BCE and contains some of the most brilliant theological teaching about the nature of God and of life ever written. The struggle between the Pandavas and the Kauravas has come to a head and a great battle is about to be fought. Arjun, one of the Pandavas is riding along the battle lines ready for war and he tells his chariot driver to stop in the centre of the battlefield. As he surveys the enemy he has to fight, he sees his family there, his great teachers and many whom he loves dearly and who also love him. He becomes filled with horror at the thought of the battle and drops his bow to his side, sits down in the chariot and tells his chariot driver that he cannot fight. However, Arjun's chariot driver is no ordinary mortal: he is Visnu, incarnated on earth in the form of Krisna in order to set right the balance of good and evil in the world. It is at this point that Krisna begins to teach Arjun about the nature of the self, about Brahman, about the paths to Brahman and about *dharma* and *moksa*. As a result of this teaching, Arjun's consciousness is expanded to the point that he is able to act according to his *dharma*. He is able to fulfil his role in life as a warrior and become an instrument in the divine purpose of ensuring the triumph of good over evil.

The *Ramayan*

The *Ramayan* is an epic loved by all Indians. Of all the Hindu literature which has emerged out of religious tradition the *Ramayan* has the greatest appeal to the everyday Hindu. Although overshadowed in literary dimensions by the other great epic, the *Mahabharat*,

> as a poem delineating the softer emotions of our everyday life the *Ramayana* sends its roots deeper into the hearts and minds of the million in India.[1]

There is a universality about the *Ramayan* which appeals to all races and nations. Gandhi regarded it as the greatest book in Hindu devotional literature and it seems to have a special appeal, notably because of its depiction of everyday domestic events and situations which appeal to rich and poor alike. As such, it became the focus of much of the devotional movement in Hinduism and was the theme taken up by generations of poets. The *Ramayan* spread to all parts of southern Asia and was represented in plays, poetry, song, art and sculpture and translated into many languages.

The *Ramayan* gives us a picture of the religious, social and political life of ancient India: it is a graphic description of the culture and civilization of the period in which it was written. The poet sets the story in a golden age of the kingdoms of Kosala and Videha, an ideal age of righteousness, justice, duty and morality. For two thousand years the story has been celebrated in temple ritual, religious festivals, at home shrines, and at places of pilgrimage, in recognition of the noblest of ages and the noblest of characters in Ram and Sita. It is therefore not surprising that the last words which Gandhi spoke before he died were 'Ram, Ram.'

The dating of the epic is highly complex. There was always a reluctance in Hinduism to commit sacred writings to written form, so there was a long period of oral tradition before the *Ramayan* was eventually written. Another reason for this complexity is that the *Ramayan* as we know it today is the result of many authors and poets who added to the work over a period of many generations. Even the original strand of the story probably drew upon a number of pre-existent folk tales about its hero Ram. The general consensus of opinion is that it was composed between the fourth and second centuries BCE with later additions up to about 300 CE, but there are widely differing views. Linguistically, and from the point of view of the religious ideas contained in the epic, a period just after the Vedic literature would suit the content of the epic well.

The original author of the *Ramayan* was the poet Valmiki, who probably lived in north-east India, the area in which most of the story is set. According to legend Valmiki was a robber who one day met a Hindu holy man who converted him to a more virtuous life. It was Valmiki who, perhaps drawing on folk traditions, wove together the original text. Later, many subsidiary stories and extra details were added.

The story of the *Ramayan* is a beautiful tale of devotion, duty and right relationships, and of *karma*. Ram and Sita are the ideal royal couple, Ram is a brave, wise and good warrior, and Sita his devoted, faithful, kind and beautiful wife. Dasaratha, king of Ayodhya, wished to hand over his throne to his son Ram, but the workings of *karma* were such that he was destined to die before this could take place. Instead of seeing his son crowned king and ruler of Ayodhya, Ram is banished to the forests, accompanied by his faithful wife and brother. There they live the lives of hermits and are befriended by the holy men who live a life of meditative retreat in the seclusion of the forest. The central episode of the long narrative is the abduction of Sita by the demon Ravan, and Ram's pursuit and rescue of her aided by the brave monkey-general Hanuman. The story has both a happy and sad ending – happy, in that Sita is rescued by Ram and returns to Ayodhya after fourteen years to be greeted by its citizens with the greatest possible joy, but sad because a probably later insertion at the end of the epic finds Sita's chastity during her period of capture by Ravan questioned for a second time. She is banished, and when she returns to Ayodhya, it is to a second trial by fire to prove her innocence. But Sita, who came out of the earth at her birth calls Mother Earth to take her back into the earth from which she came. The saintly wife of Ram is taken in the arms of her Mother and disappears forever.

The concept of *avatars*

The *Ramayan*, like the other epic the *Mahabharat*, is important because of the doctrine of *avatars*, the incarnations of God in human form. It is the God Visnu who incarnates in both epics: in the *Ramayan* he is the *avatar* Ram, the hero of the story and in the *Mahabharat* the *avatar* Krisna. The *avatars* are very important in the concept of *bhakti*, meaning 'loving devotion' to a personal deity – for, by becoming manifest in this way, Ram and Krisna have become the objects of devotion to the masses of Hindus thereby providing a more meaningful representation of the more abstract Brahman.

The Hindu concept of God is one of an ultimate Absolute which cannot be described in any way: it is *nirguna*, 'without qualities'. Everything in the universe is seen as a particle or manifestation of this Absolute so this ultimate Absolute is also *with* qualities, that is, it is *saguna*. It is *saguna* when it is everything in the universe. But the possibilities of such manifestations are endless, limitless: so Brahman can take any form, indeed already is every form. The *avatars* represent manifestations of the divine which are intermediaries between the Absolute and humankind. They represent the ideal in morality, justice, devotion to duty and perfection – the capabilities of human beings when they realize the divine particle, the *atman* within themselves.

Important in the *Ramayan* and in all scripture related to the *avatars* of Visnu, is the human nature of the *avatars*. It is this aspect which enables people to come close to them. The life of Ram, in particular, is a mixture of the divine and human, though his unawareness of his divinity throughout the narrative makes him all the more easy to relate to. And this human nature is further enhanced by his emotion, such as when he has to leave his distraught mother and hasten away because emotion overwhelms him: this episode shows that he is capable of deep suffering. We meet Ram in the *Ramayan* as a mature man who has clear characteristics of honesty and uprightness, while Sita shows kindness, obedience and chastity, characteristics which make the ideal hero and heroine to the Hindu mind. In Tulsi Das' version of the *Ramayan*, Ram's extreme sorrow in exile is portrayed by relating how he has to sleep on the ground, find roots and fruit to eat, and how he cries when Sita has an ominous dream and when he hears his father has died. Ram and Sita have to endure great hardships, but through this suffering and privation the qualities of right action come through thereby providing a model for the millions of Hindus today.

Despite the importance of this concept of *avatars* it is unlikely that Ram was thought to be an incarnation of Visnu in the original work of Valmiki. This concept is stressed in the first and last books which we know to be later additions. Ram may have been portrayed as thoroughly human in the original epic, then he became a partial incarnation and finally a full incarnation.

The *Ramayan* and the *Mahabharat* give us a thorough understanding of the concept of *dharma* – 'what is right'. Ram is the embodiment of *dharma*. So Ram and Sita are perfect examples of how man and woman should be, both individually and in their relationship with each other. The epics, then, bring the complex concept of *dharma* into real situations, in this way providing moral guidance in a very concrete form for the Hindu. 'What is right' is learnt through the characters of Ram, Sita and Lakshman rather than through philosophical speculation. Not only, then, does such *smrti* literature bring people close to God, but it also shows what is required of them at their very best.

3

Varnadharma

One aspect of Hinduism which everyone seems to have heard about is the caste system – the practice of differentiating people in society into different groups. Caste is an aspect of Hinduism which is often misunderstood. Let us, then, investigate the misconceptions and try to understand the nature of the system in India as well as the reasoning behind it. To begin with, the use of the term *caste* must be redefined. There are, in fact, two words which are used in Hindu society to refer to the various groupings of society, *varna* and *jati*. Unfortunately, writers on Hinduism rarely differentiate between the two and simply translate both as 'caste' referring to the 'caste' system of India. This is incorrect for *varna* and *jati* refer to two *different* systems and it is necessary to examine each in turn to see why the term 'caste' should be used with caution.

Varna, class

The word *varna* means 'colour' and it refers to a *religious* system of classification of people in Hinduism into four classes, dating back to the very earliest of times. In the second millennium BCE the *Aryans* invaded India and it was they who established the tradition of dividing society into four classes. Hindus would consider this four-class system to be a religious one because in one of the *Aryan* scriptures, the *Rg Veda*, there is a hymn which tells of the sacrifice of a huge primeval man called *Purusa* from whom the four classes came:

> When they divided man
> Into how many parts did they divide him?
> What was his mouth? What his arms?
> What are his thighs called? What his feet?

The Brahman was his mouth
The arms were made the Prince
His thighs the common people
And from his feet the serf was born.[1]

Thus it can be seen clearly from this hymn that society was felt to be divided into four classes: the priestly class who were the *Brahmins*; the ruling, administrative and warrior class called the *Rajanyas*, or *Ksatriyas*; the artisans, merchants, tradesmen and farmers called the *Vaisyas*; and the labourers who were the *Sudras*. The hymn from the *Rg Veda* depicts the nature of these people in symbolic and mythological imagery and this is an important point in understanding the class system of Hinduism.

The *Brahmins* are the priests who spring from the mouth, and it is the mouth which one needs for chanting the sacred scriptures: so the myth of the sacrifice of this primeval man suggests that some people are born with the capabilities for leading others in important religious ritual. When the *Aryans* first arrived in India, their scriptures were not written down but memorized by the *Brahmins* who were the only class of people capable of learning, memorizing and reciting them with precise correctness for the purpose of carrying out religious ritual and of being effective mediators between humankind and the divine. So by saying that the priestly class comes forth from the mouth of *Purusa*, the myth shows that it is the *dharma* of a *Brahmin* to be what he is. However, not all Hindu priests are *Brahmins* for there are many priests of the lower classes who carry out specific functions pertinent only to those classes. What distinguishes the former from the latter is the classical study of the *Vedas* and scholarship of the former, whereas the latter may not be very learned or educated at all. In fact, some priests are illiterate.

The myth also tells us that the arms formed the 'Prince'. This is the *Rajanya/Ksatriya class*, the people in society who are rulers like the *rajas*, the government administrators and, since rulership often involved protection of one's subjects and expansion of one's kingdom, warriors, in particular. It is the arms of *Purusa* which are needed for action, for an active way of life, so the myth shows us that it is the *dharma* of some people in life to be the protectors of others. This would be a function which a *Brahmin* could not perform because he would not have the right ingredients (of *Purusa*) in his personality to be a warrior.

The thighs of *Purusa* formed the common people, the *Vaisyas*, those in society who provide the necessary things for the rest of society to function. The thighs of the body are strong and supporting, so *Vaisyas* would have the temperament to work at more manual tasks, albeit sometimes skilled ones. But, not having the characteristics of the *Brahmin* or *Ksatriya*, they would not be able to carry out the particular responsibilities of those classes. Finally, the myth tells us, the serf is born from the feet of *Purusa* – the part of the body which supports all the other parts. So it is the *dharma* of the *Sudra*, the fourth class, to support the rest of society by acting as a servant.

What this myth is pointing out is that *religiously* people are destined to have different abilities and skills and that because the potentiality for other skills is not present, it would be useless for a *Sudra*, for example, to take on the functions of a *Brahmin*. Ideally, if society operated perfectly, each class would fulfil its own potential which would be seen as different from, but equal to, any of the other classes. The myth suggests that each class is necessary for the survival of the others and that, just as we do not despise the feet because they happen to be lower than any other part of the body, so we should not despise the *Sudra* for being the serving class in society. Ideally, we should treat all as equal but with different abilities. The early parts of the Hindu scripture, the *Ramayan*, depict very well this ideal interrelation of the four classes in the golden age of Hinduism. And while *religiously* such distinctions are made, economically it would be a mistake to believe that all *Brahmins* are priests and are wealthy or that all *Sudras* are servants and poor. *Religiously* it is only the top three classes which are *dvija*, 'twice-born', and who are able to go through a ceremony to initiate them into the stages of Hindu religious life. *Sudras* and, indeed, women, are not generally deemed to have the required characteristics of personality to be *dvija*. But *Sudras* and women, can do, and have done, well economically. Nevertheless, the village scene tends towards a more rigorous economic classification by class and caste.

Outcastes

Beyond the class system, that is to say, too low to be even ranked in the four classes are those beyond its pale, the outcastes. The Government of India Act of 1935 called them 'exterior castes' or 'scheduled castes' but Gandhi termed them *Harijans*, 'Children of God' though, rather unfortunately, the term can also mean 'love-child' or 'bastard'. They prefer to refer to themselves in today's world as *dalits* – 'the oppressed' – and their sheer numbers means that they can weild considerable political power. Some rise to political fame and there have been a number of cabinet ministers and one prime minister from the *dalit* class. But it would be true to say that, despite education to graduate and postgraduate levels, discrimination persists. Yet Killingley notes that, while some *dalits* try to rise beyond their outcaste status, others try to *claim dalit* status, because present government discrimination in favour of them can be a distinct advantage.[2]

From what has been described above, therefore, from a Hindu perspective the class system would be seen as a very logical way of viewing society. Added to this is another important perspective, the distribution of the *gunas*. Hinduism believes that everything in the cosmos is composed, in varying degrees, of three qualities called *gunas*. There are three of these *gunas* – *sattva*, *rajas*, and *tamas*. *Sattva* is light, truth, evolution, wisdom, intellect, the kind of quality which allows one to progress spiritually and to pursue what is right. Its opposite is *tamas*, which is dullness, inertia, the quality which tends to hold one back and which is averse to progress. *Rajas* is the active quality, the one which makes us go out and *do* things. Everything in life is felt to be a combination of these three *gunas* but while we have all of them in us and may experience one or another at certain times, Hindus believe that one of these *gunas* will be the dominating characteristic of each person's character, while there will be a less obvious secondary *guna*.

If we turn back now to the four classes and apply the theory of the *gunas* to them it can be seen that each class is believed to have its own characteristics from the point of view of the *gunas*. Thus:

Brahmins	*sattva – rajas*
Ksatriyas	*rajas – sattva*
Vaisyas	*rajas – tamas*
Sudras	*tamas – rajas*

Thus, the Hindu would claim that the *Vaisyas* and the *Sudras*, for example, have no *sattvic guna* and would therefore not have the kind of qualites which could carry out the pursuit of religious practice typical of a *Brahmin* who is endowed with so much *sattva*. Similarly, it is only the *Ksatriya* who has sufficient active energies, combined with the necessary wisdom, to become involved in war or administration. A *Vaisya* would have the active energy but not the wisdom to be a warrior leader.

Hindus, then, see the class system as a very logical one and feel that they simply recognize the restrictive elements that are present in all societies. To go against your class, then, is to go against your own personality, it is to try to behave like someone else when you do not have the characteristics in your personality to do so. Hindu scriptures therefore often stress that it is always better to follow one's own *dharma* than to try to live that of another.

Jati, caste

When we refer to *class* in Hinduism we are really referring to the four religiously orientated and rather ancient classes highlighted above. When we refer to *caste* we are really speaking of *jati* which means 'birth', and this is far more important for Hindus because it affects so many aspects of daily life. Whereas there are only four classes in Hinduism there are thousands of castes. Caste is not a religious institution, unlike *varna*, but is economic and geographical in origin, though it is impossible to say exactly why and how all the castes came about. While it is true to say that *jatis* are often subdivisions of *varna*, class, it would be overstating the case to say that this was the origin of the caste system as a whole. It is to *jati* that most Hindus today refer when they talk of caste and it is *jati* which really dictates the rules and regulations of life for the average Hindu. Each *jati* has its own special caste regulations in terms of food, occupation, marriage, social interaction and the like, and from each caste will come a number of sub-castes making the whole system a highly complicated one which defies examination. Castes may often be occupational but this does not preclude a member of one caste working at the occupation of another, for example in agriculture; this results in a very complex system. What we can say is that there are many *Brahmin* castes, just as there would be many *Ksatriya* or *dalit* castes, and just as the four *varnas* are hierarchically viewed, so also are the various castes within a particular *varna*.

The word caste was originally applied by the Portuguese in the sixteenth century, and since the Portuguese *casta* means 'pure' or 'chaste', it suggests very well the importance to the Hindu of maintaining the ritual and social purity of each *jati*. Important in Hindu society, too, is the idea that one does not marry outside one's *jati*; indeed, expulsion from the family and caste as a whole is likely to ensue should this happen, but it is not unusual for a whole section of a particular *jati* to separate off and adopt different dietary, ritual or occupational stances and thus become distinct.[3]

Underlying this whole concept of class and caste is the Hindu belief in *karma* and *samsara*. Because of the *karma* accumulated in past lives an individual is born into the kind of life which reflects the *karmic* balance of good or evil. So a *Brahmin* is such because of his past good *karma* from previous lives; others, whose past *karma* is sufficiently bad, may be born *outside* the caste or class system, as an *outcaste*.

4

Asramadharma

The *asramas*

In Hindu scriptures the life of an individual is conceived of as being divided into four periods of unequal time called *asramas*. The observance of the four *varnas* and the four *asramas* were important foundations in Hindu social and spiritual life, but today in modern India fewer people observe the system. A third of the Hindu population is composed of *Sudras*, the lowest class, and it would be rare for a *Sudra* to observe the four *asramas*. And although some women may observe the custom, it does not, generally, apply to women for they are religiously excluded from the *asrama* system. The observing of the four *asramas* is based on the ideal that to renounce materialism and worldly pleasures should be an important aspect of the later stages of life, for it would assist a person to achieve *moksa*, liberation from reincarnation. But while this is the overall goal, it is also realized that there must be, at some time during one's life, a period when marriage, social status and material wealth are necessary. Such aspects are catered for in the four periods and are considered essential in the experience of an individual; indeed, without them, reincarnation is thought to be inevitable. The *asramas*, then, are four distinct periods of life, the first being a period from birth to anything from 12 to 25 years of age when a male studies the Vedic scriptures and remains celibate. The second *asrama* is the period of marriage and the life of a householder, *grhastha*, the third a period of retirement and retreat in celibacy, and the fourth, total renunciation of the world.

The ideal of renunciation of materialism and marriage, and a life of celibacy, was particularly evident in about the sixth century BCE and may have influenced the institution of the *asramas* in Hinduism for, by the fifth century, there is evidence of the system in Hindu society.

However, in its beginnings, it seems that, after the first *asrama*, a young adult could choose which of the other *asramas* he would wish to pursue for the rest of his life. So, he could either remain a celibate student studying with his teacher or *guru* until he died, or he could marry, or go straight into the third or fourth *asramas*. However, in many ways this went against the traditional teaching in Hinduism concerning the importance of marriage and procreation and it was not without its critics. So the system changed to one which advocated the passage of an individual through the four *asramas* in one lifetime. This passage represents the necessary stages of life, rather like rungs of a ladder, through which one travels to ultimate liberation. While it is not expected that every Hindu should go through the four *asramas*, indeed, many never advance beyond the second, once an individual has embarked on the next *asrama* it is virtually impossible to revert back, and indeed would result in turning oneself into an outcaste.

The first *asrama*, the student

This first period of life is a time of immaturity when the Hindu is undergoing a period of formal education. He is called a *brahmachari* and is taught by his elders and is prepared by them to become a useful and mature member of society. His education will not only fit him for a future profession, but will equip him also for family, social and religious life. However, many Hindus are not prepared to live such a disciplined life for a long period and some cannot afford such a formal education at all. So the first *asrama* has shrunk to between 12 and 15 years. This is even the case for many *Brahmins*.

The second *asrama*, the householder

This is the householder, *grhastha*, stage – the undertaking of marriage and the duties of raising and supporting a family. It is a measure of the importance of the family in Hinduism that the earlier idea of missing out this *asrama* in order to remain a celibate student, hermit in retreat, or wandering recluse, did not gain ground. Hindus always felt it important to raise a family and even today, despite immense poverty, a couple will continue to have many children, at least until a boy is born. During the householder stage it is expected that a man should work at a trade or profession to support his family, but also to contribute to the welfare of the community. Hinduism is perhaps unique in suggesting that the pursuit of wealth is a *necessary* goal in life at some stage. We could include here also the idea that pleasure (*kama*) is also a goal permissable at this stage of life. Though this always seems strange to the Westerner, we should remember that the Hindu is always subject to the laws of *karma* and *dharma* and that these two concepts ideally prevent the pursuit of the kind of pleasure which would be against social and cosmic norms. The vast majority of Hindus would be very reluctant to give up this householder stage and so it usually lasts a lifetime!

The third *asrama*, the forest hermit

Traditionally, when a man becomes a grandfather, when his hair turns gray and his skin becomes wrinkled, when his children have grown up and are establishing lives of their own, then the duty of the man as a householder is at an end. In this third *asrama* the man is expected to retire from family and social life, give up his work, wealth and possessions and retreat to the forest as a forest hermit, a *vanaprastha*, to live a more spiritual life. Physical, social, material and sexual pleasures are renounced, although in some cases a wife could accompany her husband into retirement. Little contact, if any, would be maintained with other members of the family; the life would be that of the celibate recluse, though at times advice may be sought of the recluse from family and friends. In view of the denials which this kind of life brings, it is not difficult to see why the third *asrama* has become obsolete for all but a few.

The fourth *asrama*, the wandering ascetic

The fourth *asrama* is when, in late life, a Hindu renounces the world, even his wife, his social duties and his religious obligations. All desires, hopes, fears and responsibilities are abandoned and his concentration is devoted to merging with God. This is the *sannyasin* who even today in India is treated with the greatest of respect, mingled with a certain degree of fear as well as scepticism. On taking up the life of the ascetic, such men will often burn an effigy of their bodies to show that they have died to the world.

Although these four *asramas* are now not widely practised they have remained an important ideal in Hindu religious tradition, comparable to the four *varnas*. In fact, they are so important that they rank as one of the two pillars of Hindu socio-religious tradition, the other being *varna*. The two are therefore often combined together as one *dharmic* basis of Hinduism – *varnasramadharma*. As we saw earlier, the term *Hinduism* is not really a very apposite one and is really one which has been assigned to Hindu religion from outside India. If we were to ask ordinary village Hindus to say what their understanding of Hinduism is they would more than likely reply *varnasramadharma*. This really sums up everyday life in Hinduism very well – doing what is right according to your class or caste and your particular role in life.

5

Gods and Goddesses

Manifestations of Brahman

Hinduism believes that there is one, ultimate Absolute called Brahman which cannot be described in any way in its unmanifest form. But because everything in the cosmos comes forth from Brahman then the cosmos itself, and anything in it, is a *manifestation* of Brahman. It is *manifestations* of Brahman which we can describe either in the myriad forms which we see in daily life or in the form of the many Gods and Goddesses of Hinduism. 'Hinduism' is rather difficult to define and the word is not one which Hindus themselves would use partly because of the multiplicity of ideas and beliefs which can be found under this umbrella term. So if the concept that the manifestations of Brahman in the universe are infinite is combined with the idea that the level of consciousness and personal evolution of each individual is different and will necessitate different views of divinity, the result is a multiplicity of Gods and Goddesses: each individual, each caste, each village, parts of villages and so on are able to worship the particular manifestation of Brahman which suits their own temperament and circumstances.

So within Hinduism it would be impossible to say how many particular Gods and Goddesses there are. In some cases the same God is worshipped under different names in different parts of India and most villages have their own local deities which would not be known elsewhere. Yet despite this multiplicity of Gods and Goddesses, most Hindus would certainly not regard themselves as polytheists. This is for two reasons: first, because all deities are manifestations of one Ultimate, Brahman, and secondly, because many Hindus would only worship one major deity anyway, regarding all the other deities as those which are worshipped only on certain occasions. Many of these deities are perhaps what we would call minor deities and we might want to use a small g rather than a capital one to refer to such gods and goddesses; it would depend on whether the deity is regarded as *being* Brahman (in which case a capital *G* would be correct) or just a divine being which is not directly or totally identified as Brahman. In the former case, the God would be called *Isvara* 'Lord' whereas the ordinary god and goddess are *deva* (male) and *devi* (female) respectively.

It is sometimes difficult for Westerners to understand why people should wish to worship the divine in female form. The Western religious tradition sprang from patriarchal roots; if we think back to biblical times, the early Hebrews were nomadic people, led by the head male of the tribe, so it would be natural to view their deity as male, too. Indian early history is different; there, the village scene and agriculture was paramount from the beginning, so there was an emphasis on fertility, creating a more natural tendency to view the deity in female form. Interestingly, while Hindu scriptures tend to stress the importance of the male deities, in practice, in many parts of India, female deities tend to be more revered. This is because the Hindu scriptures came into India with the Aryans, the nomadic tribes who imposed their more patriarchal views on the indigenous population, but the indigenous population itself never really lost the inclination to worship the Mother Goddess and in southern parts of India, where the Aryan influence barely reached, this predominance of female divinity worship is very strong.

Hinduism accepts a triad of three Gods – Visnu, Siva and Brahma. While these are their major names, each deity, especially the first two, is known also by many other names, according to a particular locality and the particular myths associated with the deity. The same deity, for example Visnu, may take on the aspect of different gods with different names, but as the triad the three are sometimes depicted as one God with three heads, an image which is called the *Trimurti*, meaning 'three-form'. They represent the three *gunas* which were previously discussed in the context of *varna*: Visnu represents the *sattva guna*, Siva represents the *tamas guna*, and Brahma the *rajas guna*. Of the three, Visnu and Siva are by far the most important: although the form of Brahma may be found in Hindu temples, he is rarely worshipped independently and he is, in fact, worshipped at only two temples in India.

Visnu 'The Pervader'

For Vaisnavites, the followers of Visnu, Visnu is the Supreme Brahman in manifest form. One of the most attractive features of the majority of Hindu deities is their portrayal in very pleasant forms – handsome, colourful, happy and radiant. Visnu is certainly portrayed in this way. Yet behind the outward appearance of the deities is always profound symbolism – as in all Hinduism – and this is so with Visnu. He himself symbolizes the preserving and pervading energies of life, the centripetal forces which bind atoms together to make life and evolution possible. Yet he is always depicted as dark blue, symbolizing that although he brings and sustains life, death is always the outcome of birth. Every article of his clothing and being symbolizes some aspect of the cosmos, so that whatever one looks at in looking at his image one can contemplate the more abstract ideas beyond the outward object: these are all aids to devotion. Ultimately, Visnu is pointing beyond his manifest self to the Unmanifest Brahman.

There are many legends associated with Visnu and he is often identified, in varying degrees, with other divine or mythical beings. For example, Visnu is sometimes equated with Purusa, the cosmic person who gave rise to the four classes and the whole universe. In particular, Visnu is often worshipped as Narayan and especially as Krisna of whom more will be said below. Once one becomes familiar with Hindu deities it is easy to recognize them by their distinct characteristics and dress. Like many of the deities, Visnu is portrayed as having four arms, a symbol of his superhuman powers and the ability to extend that power in all directions. He carries a discus, a conch, a club and a lotus (or sometimes a bow). He is also portrayed as having a special lock of hair on his chest, symbolic of his lordship over the world. To some of his worshippers he is more popularly known as Kesava, Govinda or Madhava, though these are only a few of his names for Visnu will be worshipped under a different name at most of his major temples.

Many people support the view that humankind needs a tangible, manifest and anthropomorphic conception of God to worship. It is difficult, if not impossible, to worship a formless *It* which is why manifested aspects of Brahman are so important within Hinduism. Nowhere in any religion is this more evident than with the incarnation of a God in human form and one of the reasons why Vaisnavism is so popular in Hinduism is because Visnu, as we have seen, is said to have incarnated himself on earth a number of times. Though the number of incarnations varies in the different texts, two stand out as being of paramount importance in Hindu worship – the incarnations or *avatars* of Visnu as Ram and as Krisna. The *avatar* of Ram has been dealt with in some detail in the context of the *Ramayan* and now we need to look at Krisna.

Krisna

The stories about Krisna are immensely attractive to all Hindus. Like the *Ramayan* they tell of jealousies and battles, of love and intrigue and, essentially, of the eventual triumph of good over evil. Krisna was born on earth so that the balance of good in the world could be restored, hence the many stories involving Krisna see him overcoming evil demons and people. His very birth epitomizes the evil state of the world, for his parents, Prince Vasudeva and Princess Devaki, had been imprisoned by the wicked demon king Kamsa because he had been told that their eighth child would bring about his death. Despite Kamsa being able to kill six of their children, Krisna and his brother were transferred to safety in the village of Gokula 'Cow-village' and were raised by foster parents. It was in this village that Krisna was given his name which, in view of his dark blue colour, means 'black'.

There are many beautiful stories about Krisna's babyhood and youth which appeal to Hindus of all ages. The stories show the baby or young Krisna in earthly form yet at the same time depict Krisna as the ultimate Lord of the Universe. On one occasion, Yasoda, Krisna's foster mother, wanted to punish him for putting earth in his mouth, but when she looked inside his mouth to try to get it out she saw the whole universe in it! On another occasion Krisna, who, it seems, had a considerable partiality for butter, had stolen his mother's butter for the umpteenth time. Exasperated, Yasoda tried to catch her child and tie him up, but he could not be caught, for who can bind God or hold God in their hands? Even as an infant, however, Krisna, unlike Ram, is depicted as being thoroughly aware of his total identity with Visnu and there is never any suggestion of duality between the two. He is sufficiently aware of why his foster mother is unable to bind him and allows her to do so only out of pity.

What is particularly attractive about the stories of Krisna as a young man and his life among the villagers is the classlessness of them: here is a divine being living among ordinary mortals in everyday village life. We hear about the pranks he plays on his fellow cowherds and cowherdesses, even to the extent of stealing the girls' clothes while they are bathing in the river! While we are never allowed to forget that Krisna is a divine being, he is also full of fun, confidence, and above all, love. It is this last aspect which is very important on the symbolic level. Outwardly, the *gopis*, the cowherdesses, were all in love with Krisna, but he had a favourite, Radha. His love affair with Radha symbolizes the love of the human soul for God and, equally, God's love for humankind. The ardent love of the *gopis* for Krisna symbolizes the devotee who can love God to the same extent, so devoted to God that the personal self, the ego, is lost. This is the height of devotional Hinduism, called *bhakti*. Strictly speaking, *bhakti* should transcend class barriers for Krisna was a *Ksatriya* while Radha was a low-caste *gopi*. But in practice, devotional Hinduism has also accommodated the inequalities of caste.

As had been foretold, Krisna returned to his place of birth and killed Kamsa, freeing his parents and setting up the rightful kingdom of his own family. Although he had to leave the village of his childhood and the many friends who loved him he assured them all that as long as they kept him firmly in mind at all times and remained devoted to him, then he would always be with them. This symbolizes the idea that God is always with his *bhakta*, his loving devotee. What is so special about Krisna is that he can be worshipped in any of the forms previously mentioned, as a baby, as a youth, as a lover, as a lord, or even as the great God Visnu. Again, it depends on the nature of the individual in which way he or she wishes to pour out devotion to this versatile God.

Siva 'The Auspicious'

Known by many names (Mahadeva, Bhava, Nataraja, Mahayogi, Bhairava, Pasupati, Visvanat, to name only a few), Siva is probably the most complicated of Hindu deities: indeed, even Hindus themselves recognize this by putting his shrine in the temple separate from those of other deities. In order to convey the mystery and transcendency of Siva it is more usual to find his symbol in temples. This symbol is the *linga*, which is a phallic symbol, but one should not make the mistake of seeing this as a mere sexual image. In Hinduism symbols on our phenomenal level point to some profound truth on the cosmic level and this is what the *linga* does. It represents the energies necessary for life on both the microcosmic level – the world in which we live – and on the macrocosmic level, the level of the whole cosmos, the level at which Brahman becomes manifest in the whole of the universe. In a

Saivite temple, the *linga* would be placed right in the centre, underneath the spire, where it symbolizes the centre, the navel of the earth.

Sometimes, however, it is possible to see the actual image of Siva in a temple. His hair will be piled high on the top of his head and in it will be the moon. From his hair tumbles the river Ganges, the most sacred river in Hinduism. Tradition states that Siva allowed the Ganges to fall upon earth from his own hair to save the destruction it would have caused had nothing broken its fall. His throat is blue because at one time, when the ocean was being churned by the gods and demons, a deadly poison came to the surface. Only a God as great as Siva and to whom life and death are equal, could swallow this poison without harm, and this Siva does. The story thus tells us that he is beyond all the opposites of life, even death itself. Though not always portrayed as such, Siva has three eyes, an extra one in the middle of his forehead which depicts his omniscient, all-knowing, nature. Around his neck is a coiled serpent representing *kundalini*, the spiritual energy within life. Unlike Visnu, Siva is depicted as white as snow. This is because, although he is primarily the dissolving force in life, the one which works against creation, death will always bring life, because of the cycle of *samsara*: one has to die in order to be reborn. So although Siva is depicted as the Dissolver in life, the one who brings death, it is death which is the medium for the transformation into a new life, a new creation. Siva dissolves in order to create: this portrays clearly the opposites of life and death and destruction and creation in his character. It is because of his responsibility for death and dissolution that Siva symbolizes the *tamas guna*, the centrifugal force of the universe. Because he brings life through death his name Siva means 'Bright One', 'Happy One', or 'Auspicious One'. Siva is often depicted riding a bull called Nandi and in Saivite temples Nandi, decked in garlands and chains, can usually be found just outside the shrine of Siva facing the *linga*, like a doorkeeper.

Siva is often portrayed as the supreme ascetic, very still, passive and utterly calm, but because he is a God of opposites he always has within him the potential for quite the opposite, a ferocious and terrible aspect. It is this aspect of Siva which is noticeable in the earlier periods of Hinduism. Although a very complicated deity to understand, Siva is one of the most fascinating. To his devotees, he is seen as Brahman, the Absolute and it is not difficult to see why because just as all opposites are united in the unmanifest Absolute so also are they united in the manifest Siva.

Ganesh

A lesser God, but a very important one, is Ganesh, one of the sons of Siva. His name means 'Lord' (*isha*) 'of attendants' (*ganas*). He is easily recognized because he has the head of an elephant. There are various stories which suggest how he acquired his head. Perhaps the main one tells of a time when Siva was away for many years and returned to find a youth guarding his wife Parvati's room. When the youth refused to allow Siva to enter her room, Siva cut off his head, only to find that he had killlled his own son. To calm Parvati's obvious distress, he ordered the head of the first thing to be found to be placed on his son's body but in obeying this command to the letter, his attendant returned with the head of an elephant! Parvati was not very pleased with the result! To offset this, it was decreed that Ganesh would be the bringer of good fortune to many worshippers, should be worshipped before all other gods could be worshipped, except Siva, and would be the medium for overcoming all obstacles. So anyone beginning a business, writing an examination paper, getting married and so on, would always worship Ganesh first. He is thus *very* popular all over India and is even found in remote cave shrines in Indonesia.

The Mother Goddess

Perhaps the one word which is helpful in understanding the many complexities of most Eastern religions is *equilibrium*. In a state of equilibrium, one is neither this nor that, one simply *is* and this would be *moksa* for the Hindu. But manifest existence is not in a state of equilibrium; it is full of dualities, called *dvandva* in Sanskrit. So we have good and evil, light and dark, peace and war and so on, and we also have male and female. Whatever is manifest in life is subject to these dualities and this is so on the macrocosmic level too. So Hindus would find it very strange to conceive of divinity as only *one* side of the duality of male and female: Brahman is the *equilibrium* between all opposites and is unmanifest, but once Brahman is manifest in divine beings, it would not be logical for manifestation to be just male. Indeed, if there is any differentiation of importance between male and female deities on the macrocosmic level, or between male and female on the microcosmic level – the world of humankind – it is more the result of cultural practice than of metaphysical reasoning.

It is because of this idea of equilibrium that each manifestation of Brahman in divine form must be both male and female. The female side of each of the male deities is called the *sakti* force. It is usually the active energy of the God, while the male side is the more passive form. Sometimes the male or female aspect of the deity will be worshipped separately depending on which is the most important to the individual worshipper. We should always remember that in Hinduism there are a multiplicity of paths to God, like the different fingers pointing to the same moon, which we noted at the outset.

Worship of a Mother Goddess has been part of Indian tradition since its earliest times and it was only when the Aryan invaders brought a more patriarchal religion that the balance between male and female deities seems to have been upset. But life in Indian villages is very slow to change and has hardly changed at all in some, so that although the Sanskrit scriptures may well show a favouritism for worshipping male deities and often depict female goddesses as inferior, in the life of the villages, the goddess often remains paramount. While the word for goddess is *devi*, the more popular name for the goddess is *mata* or *amma*, both meaning 'mother', and the names of many female deities are compounded with these or other forms to indicate a concept of the divine as Mother.

Laksmi

Each of the major Gods of the *Trimurti*, then, has his female counterpart. The counterpart of Visnu is the Goddess Laksmi who is sometimes called Sri, though originally these were two different goddesses. Laksmi is the symbol of good fortune and prosperity in life, and like her consort Visnu she is an omnipresent and eternal being. Like Visnu she has four arms, in one of which she carries a lotus blossom, the symbol of the enlightened soul of each human being. In another of her hands she carries coins which are often depicted as falling from her hand, showing that she bestows blessings. According to one myth, gods and demons combined together to churn the ocean to obtain a nectar of immortality, and during the churning process, Laksmi rose from it in order to take care of the welfare of the earth. At that time, Visnu became present on earth in the form of a huge tortoise. Whenever Visnu comes to earth as an *avatar*, Laksmi accompanies him. Thus she, too, becomes an *avatar*: she is Sita, the wife of Ram in the *Ramayan* and she is Radha, the favourite *gopi* of Krisna.

Laksmi is the *active* energy of Visnu, so while Visnu is creator, Laksmi *is* creation. While Visnu supports and sustains the earth, Laksmi *is* the earth and identifiable with all females on it in the same way that Visnu is identifiable with all males. Visnu is speech, while Laksmi is meaning; Visnu is understanding while Laksmi is intellect; Laksmi is the creeping vine, Visnu the tree to which it clings; Visnu is love, and Laksmi is pleasure. There is a profound interaction between the two, it is as if Visnu is the thought behind the universe and Laksmi is the one who puts the thought into action. This is how the *sakti* force operates in all the male deities. Because of their inseparability, Laksmi and Visnu are known as Laksmi-Narayan, a name which designates them as a personal manifestation of Brahman: in whatever state Visnu appears, divine or mortal, Laksmi will always be with him and the interdependence of the two is often depicted in images which combine their two forms into one, Visnu constituting the right half and Laksmi the left.

Laksmi is one of the most popular Goddesses in India and is very widely worshipped by people of all castes. She is closely associated with right conduct, truth, generosity and social order, and she likes personal and environmental cleanliness. Those wishing to attract her benevolence at certain festivals, therefore, have to make sure their homes are scrupulously clean. Just as she was a model wife as Sita in the *Ramayan* so she is a model consort to, and complement of, Visnu.

The *sakti* aspects of Siva: Parvati

As we might expect in view of the complicated nature of the God Siva, his *sakti* energies are very complex indeed. He does not have one consort, but many, and these rather suit the opposite natures of his own personality, mild and gentle on the one side and ferocious and terrible on the other, offering life on the one hand and death on the other and so on. If we look first at the gentler aspects, these are personified in Parvati and Uma. Parvati means 'Daughter of the Mountain' and reflects her birth from the Himalayan mountain range. It is in the form of Parvati that the Goddess is the constant companion of her consort Siva; accounts of her in independent exploits, apart from the intimate relation between the two, are sparse. The role of Parvati as the consort of Siva is to balance his ascetic, passive and reclusive nature by making him more involved in the world so most of the stories about Parvati are concerned with luring him into marriage or of recounting how helpless he is without his *sakti* energy. So Parvati is really an ideal domesticated wife, the perfect wife and mother. She is not worshipped as an independent Goddess.

Uma

Uma is really the original consort of Siva. Because he is sometimes called Mahadeva 'Great God' she is sometimes called Devi and at other times Sati. She was the daughter of Brahma who opposed her marriage to the great ascetic God Siva. When Brahma refused to attend a great sacrificial celebration arranged by her husband, Uma flung herself in the sacrificial fires and died. It is because of her self immolation here, showing her utter devotion to her husband, that the practice of *sati*, the voluntary burning of a widow on her husband's funeral pyre, became common in India and is still practised occasionally today. But Sati could not be separated from her consort and was eventually born in earthly form and reunited with her husband as Parvati.

Durga

The name Durga means 'Inaccessible' and here we see immediately, the very active side of this *sakti* energy of the God Siva. Durga is usually portrayed riding a lion or tiger and killing a buffalo-demon. Being composed of the angry energies of all the male gods, there is nothing gentle about this image, for she is a ferocious protector of the good and faithful. She carries weapons, held in her many arms, of a trident, a sword, a bow, and a discus. Despite her fierce nature, she is immensely popular in India for her impressive role in destroying evil. She probably has links with the early goddess worship associated with fertility for her main festival occurs at the time of the harvest and she is associated with crops and plants. Animal sacrifice, often associated with fertility rites, is still offered to her. Durga can take many forms but the most well known is probably that of Kali.

Kali

Kali is the most terrifying of the *sakti* forces of Siva. The name means 'Black' and, indeed, she is associated with the darker sides of life. In her worst form she is portrayed as dancing in cremation grounds and as drinking blood, and thousands of goats are still sacrificed to her at the Kalighat temple in Calcutta as well as in smaller temples and shrines elsewhere. But despite her cruel image, her devotees worship her as the divine Mother, for it is Kali who releases humankind from *samsara*: indeed, that is why she is associated with cremation grounds, for it is only through accepting death that we can hope to be reborn and only by letting go of this world and losing the ego, the personality self, that we can realize *moksa*. Kali, indeed, is depicted as overcoming the kind of enemies which would daunt even the bravest of gods. Once, in attempting to slay a giant, she found that every drop of blood which came from the giant produced another thousand of them. Her only recourse was to drink its blood as she slew him. This is why Kali is usually shown with her tongue hanging out and blood dripping from it. Like many of the Gods she has four arms, and in one she carries a sword and in the other the head of the giant. Her earrings are two dead bodies, her necklace is made of skulls and she is dressed only in a girdle of dead mens' hands. She has red eyes and a body smeared with blood – no wonder her devotees feel protected!

Space limitations allow only a few of the major female deities to be outlined here but there are countless others, particularly in the southern parts of India where worship of the female divinities is far more popular than the male ones. Village goddesses are a particularly fascinating study for the function of these goddesses is to protect the village – to guard the inhabitants from smallpox, for example (though this disease has now declined in India). These local goddesses have little cosmic function but more of a local, existential one. In fact, in an Indian village these local deities would be far more important than the great deities of Hinduism. Because of this it is not impossible for new goddesses to emerge: Santosi Ma 'Mother of Satisfaction' is a case in point; she is rapidly becoming a goddess of such importance that she may be incorporated in the major pantheon of deities in time.[1] The cult of Santosi Ma has gained currency in the last forty years or so in northern India and while the origins of the goddess are obscure she has been declared to be an offspring of the deity Ganesh, of the genealogical line of Siva. In 1975 a film was made about her as a result of which Santosi Ma has become immensely popular. She is a good example of a modern goddess, one who serves the immediate needs of the people, who *satisfies* their needs and who is readily accessible to her devotees. Brand comments rather appropriately:

> Perhaps one reason behind Santosi Mata's astonishing rise to fame is that it was simply felt inappropriate to ask an ancient goddess for such modern appliances as radios and refrigerators.[2]

Certainly, worship of the female goddess is an important aspect of Hindu religion and in some cases all the female deities are absorbed into one great Mother Goddess, Mahadevi 'Great Goddess', who is worshipped as the ultimate manifestation of Brahman. But at the local level, village goddesses are felt to be more appropriate to the needs of every day life.

So at one end of the scale we have the great Gods and Goddesses who symbolize the cosmic energies of the universe and at the other, the *gramadevatas* or village deities so important in the daily life of the village Hindu, who relate much more pertinently to the life of the individual, family and caste. There are many important deities which have not been mentioned, in particular a whole host of earlier Vedic deities who still feature in the myths of present-day Hinduism, many of whom are precursors of the greatest of the present-day Gods. What is important is that the individual is able to relate to the divine in the form which best suits his or her level of consciousness and individual circumstances: the paths to the divine are endless.

6

Worship in the Home and Temple

Worship of the divine in Hinduism, whether it be formal national or local festivals, at temple, outdoor shrine, or home shrine, is characterized by immense diversity. The very nature of Hinduism with its multiplicity of approaches to, and aspects of, the divine, facilitates this. Worship in Hinduism is a *daily* event, whether performed at home or at a temple or outdoor shrine. It is *nitya*, 'obligatory', for a practising Hindu. Such daily worship is called *puja*, a word which is not so easily translated since it has connotations of respect, honour, and veneration and therefore can be directed to parents, to one's teacher, one's *guru*, or to a holy man, as well as to a god or goddess.

Images

Most people associate Hinduism with a multiplicity of deities which are represented in the form of images. The word *idols* is often used by Westerners in depicting such images, but there is a nuance of thought between the two words which makes 'image' far more appropriate. Westerners use the term 'idol' to suggest that it is the statue or idol itself which is worshipped, and nothing beyond it. 'Image', on the other hand, suggests an image *of* something, and can therefore be representative of, or symbolic for, something beyond the visible form. This is an idea more appropriate to Hinduism, in which forms are but a manifestation of a formless Absolute. The term 'idol', therefore, is partly incorrect, and in some Western senses could be said to be offensive. A Hindu would generally use the term *murti* to indicate the image of a deity and the way in which a *murti* is viewed by individuals would vary considerably. Many Hindus regard the *murtis* as representations of the deities, rather like a photograph represents a person. We can be very nostalgic about photographs, they can arouse emotive responses, but photographs project the mind to the reality *beyond* the print, no one identifies the photographic image as the *real* person. In the same way it could be said that a *murti* projects the mind of the worshipper to the greater essence of divinity beyond the immediate emotive representation. Thus, anthropomorphic representations of deities are by no means the norm in worship – a brass pot, a stone, or a *linga* of the deity Siva, will symbolize the power of the respective deity.

Having said this, a *murti* is often regarded as a manifestation of the presence of the *power* of a deity, something of the essence or spirit of the deity which is manifest in the world. It is in this sense that the *murti* is more directly representative of the deity itself, for the power or essence of the deity is believed to be *in* the *murti*, either temporarily, as for some festivals, or permanently, as in some temple images. But in containing a deity's power or essence, there is little suggestion that this *is* the deity in its entirety: more usually, the deity itself is conceived of as being beyond its manifestation of power in the *murti* and not confined by it. In many senses, all aspects of manifest existence are ultimately Brahman, so any image of a deity can be identified as such. Either way, *murtis* are treated as if they are royalty and suggest the presence of the deity at the *puja* proceedings. Great care is therefore important in conducting *puja*, particularly the maintaining of purity and in terms of the regular, daily washing, dressing, and approaching of the deities. *Murtis* are specially consecrated in a ceremony called *pratistha* before they can be the focus of *puja* whether at home or in the temple, and an old or damaged *murti* is always thrown into the sea to dipose of it. Frequently, symbols serve the purpose of locating the deity, or the power of the deity. A *kalas* will often be seen. It is a small brass pot containing water, curds and ghee and has a coconut on top. This is a typical representation of a form of the goddess, sometimes being placed beneath a picture of her. The great God Siva has both an anthropomorphic form and the powerful symbol of the *linga*, the phallic symbol which represents the potent energy which is manifest in the cosmos. It is also important to recognize that it is not the great Gods of Hinduism but the ordinary deities, especially village deities and what they symbolize, which are important to many Hindus, particularly those of lower castes.[1] The major deities such as Visnu and Siva are considered to be uninterested in the daily events of the ordinary man or woman.

Other objects of worship

If the essence of Brahman is in all things, then all things in life have a basic sacredness. However, Hindus generally single out certain species of animals and vegetation. The pipal and banyan trees are especially sacred and are often the objects of *puja*. The *tulsi* plant (basil) is a frequent object of *puja* in the home, for it is connected with the deity Visnu. Animals are also considered to be sacred, the cow being the most well known. While not actually worshipped, it is respected and venerated as a sacred animal and is allowed to roam unharmed. Many will touch its back as they pass it, but it has to be said that Gandhi became a vegetarian because he felt cows were ill-treated. Such is the respect for the cow that Indians have offered to take in the millions of cows waiting for slaughter in Britain as a result of the present crisis in beef production.[2] Snakes, while feared, are also venerated in India, and Hindu mythology features them widely. Monkeys are also venerated and may be allowed to roam free in some temples. Despite their sacred nature, they sometimes bite! At some festival occasions, even the tools of one's trade may be the object of *puja*, and what appears to be an ordinary stone is in fact a representation of a female divinity in many shrines. In many instances the object of veneration is a symbol or representation of the deity or divine power beyond it.

Significant aspects of *puja*

The deity, represented by the *murti* or picture or other symbol, is considered to be an important guest, a royal guest, and is treated as such throughout *puja* with adoration, attention, care and entertainment. Purification is essential, and it would be usual to bathe in running water before performing *puja*. But in any case, a little water is sipped three times by the worshipper before performing *puja* in order to indicate purity. Washing the *murti* is essential, for a royal guest would need water to bathe after arriving from a long journey. Sometimes the washing is merely symbolic – a flower dipped gently in water is lightly touched on the face of the deity. It is the face, teeth and particularly the feet which are 'washed', just as a guest would need after travelling through the dusty streets of India. Dressing the deity is also important and the clothes chosen are bright, beautiful and often embroidered with gold-coloured threads. Ornaments are also placed on the *murti* as well as flower garlands, perfumes and oils – again, the kind of gifts one would wish to convey to a royal guest. Since the deity remains at a temple, it is both woken up in the morning and its 'needs' attended to, and put to rest at night with equal care.

Food is also important: cooked rice, fruit, ghee, sugar and betel leaf are the main types of food offered. Offering food is a very important way of honouring the deity. In Indonesia the Hindu women make elaborate pyramids of food (the wealthier they are, the higher the pyramid) which may be two or three metres high, and which are carried to the temple on the head as an offering to the deity. Such food is meticulously prepared and arranged. A cooked chicken will be splayed somewhere in the pyramid, surrounded by rice dishes and an abundance of fruit. The pyramid of food is left at the temple, to be collected later in the day. This is an important factor in all Hindu *puja*. The deity is believed to take the essence of the food, and the leftovers (*jutha*) are given back to the worshipper as what is known as *prasad*. This is a sign of grace from the deity to the worshipper. In Indonesia, the food (including the cooked chicken) is left exposed to the sun (and sometimes monsoon rains) for much of the day before being collected as *prasad*.

Fragrance and light are also offered the deity, fragrance in the form of incense sticks, and light in the form of a burning lamp usually made from a burning wick placed in ghee, which is waved before the deity. The deity is honoured in a number of ways: by applying a *tilak* to the spot between the eyebrows of the deity, the worshipper indicates awareness of the spiritual purity of the deity which, in turn, is passed to the worshipper. The worshipper may also entertain the deity with *bhajans*, hymns which offer praise and honour. This is a feature of temple *puja* in particular, as well as the home shrine, but it is possible to see groups of people singing *bhajans* on the verandahs of the temples in the evenings, having come together specifically and informally for this purpose. This may occur once or twice a week, the company usually consisting of males, though occasionally women will join in but sit separately.

The standard way of showing respect to someone in India is by means of bowing (*pranama*) and, practically, the more respect one wishes to show, the lower the bow. In the case of a deity, or a royal person, total prostration is in order. *Anjali* consists of bringing the palms together and raising them to the forehead, and combined with the bow are the actions normally used in greeting in India. The words *Namaskar* (Sanskrit) or *Namaste* (Hindi) 'I bow to you' are spoken as this is done, and these words, *anjali*, and the bow are indicative of recognition of the divine *atman* in the other person, the part of all individuals which is the same as oneself. Thus, there is a special link between the worshipper and the deity when this is done in *puja*. Since famous *gurus* are honoured in *puja*, people might touch their feet in respect, or remove the dust from a *guru's* feet before touching their own head, so indicating that the feet of the *guru* are purer than the head of the one paying respect.

Darsan

The point of *puja* in Hinduism is *darsan*, a word which means 'audience', 'viewing' or 'sight of', the object here being the deity. This is rather like gaining audience to a royal personage, the result of which is the grace of that person being bestowed on the visitor. It is the requested audience with the deity which is represented by the ringing of a bell by the worshipper at a temple or, indeed, at a home shrine. The bell summons the deity as much as announcing the arrival of the worshipper. *Darsan* might involve sitting cross-legged on the floor (but not with the soles of the feet pointed towards the deity) or, preferably, circumambulation of the *murti*. This latter is always done in a clockwise direction so that the right hand faces the deity and not the left hand, the latter being associated with all the unpleasant tasks of life. While circumambulation is desired for *darsan* it is not obligatory; indeed, it would be impossible at shrines in most homes. *Darsan* is felt to be most auspicious first thing in the morning when the deities have only just been woken up.

Puja in the home

The home is the most popular place for *puja* for it is not obligatory for people to visit the temples. Women have a great deal of freedom in religious practice in the home and it is the head woman of a household who would normally conduct *puja*. *Puja* in the home is a daily occurrence and there will usually be a small shrine set aside somewhere. A Hindu friend utilizes the stairs in her flat which had once lead to an upper floor, but, being converted into flats, the six or seven stairs lead to a blank wall. It is an ideal tiered setting to put the family deities, particularly Krisna, who is her favourite deity, and a picture of her deceased mother who had been instrumental in founding the local *mandal*, the Hindu temple, is nearby. Hindu home shrines are usually colourful, bright, and characterized by the small offerings of food, water, fragrance and light.

Sometimes, *murtis* or prints of deities are found in other parts of the home away from the main shrine, the only exception being the bathroom and toilet which are ritually unclean rooms. Westerners are often surprised to find the main shrine in the kitchen. Indeed, this is a very popular place for the family shrine, because it is always kept ritually clean. Preparation of food is very important in Hinduism and is responsible for much class/caste division. A person is felt to be impure if he or she comes into contact with impure food, so its preparation is meticulous. Shoes are never worn in the kitchen, so polluting leather, or the dust from the outside world is not allowed to enter its environs. To place a shrine in such a meticulously maintained room is common sense, so it may be that the family shrine will be located on the top of the washing machine. Sometimes the *murtis* are kept behind the closed doors of a cabinet, or closed curtains, which are opened for *puja*. Shrines will hold not only the household's chosen deities, but other deities also. There may be pictures of immediate ancestors, specially produced and highly colourful prints of deities, and pictures of modern *gurus* such as Sai Baba. It is possible that the particular deities chosen by a family may be caste specific.[3]

Puja in the temple

Although the home has always been considered the focal point for most ceremonies, many Hindus call at their local temple, the *mandir*, whenever possible: the belief is that no image should be left unworshipped for a whole day. Gifts pour into the temples, and when costly food cannot be prepared for the deity, poor people will bring grains of rice or a lump of sugar. Strictly speaking, because Hindus believe that Brahman is everywhere, it can be worshipped anywhere, so a river bank, forest grove, mountain top, or even a cowshed is a sacred place. But temples have been set up on special sites which are held to be auspiciously connected with a particular deity. However, temples are far more prolific in southern India than in the north.

The aspects which are most arresting in a Hindu temple are those which affect the senses – the colours, the sounds, the smells. The shrine or shrines within a temple house the *murtis*, the deities being dressed in brightly coloured clothes, sparkling jewellery and coloured garlands. Large temples are often highly decorated with tinsel, colourfully designed symbols and the whole atmosphere is impressively bright. The sound of bells ringing, drums being beaten, *bhajans* being sung with the worshippers clapping their hands to the rhythm accompanied by small percussion musical instruments, all serve to make the temple very much alive with activity, while the smell of incense pervades the whole building. Temples can be any shape or size, some being not larger than a cupboard, though there are distinct patterns of temples in the northern parts of India which are different in the south. But all will have three features – a representation of the deity in the form of a *murti* or symbol of the deity, a canopy over the deity in order to honour it, and a priest who cares for the sacred image and who gives each worshipper *prasad*, a gift from the deity. There are likely to be several *murtis* in some temples, but the main deity will be housed in the womb of the temple, the *garbagriha*, literally 'womb-house', over which is a tower or spire. The *garbagriha* is the inner sanctuary of the temple which is entered only by a priest. Interestingly, there is a difference between the deity in a temple and the *same* deity in the home, the former being the more powerful: the kind of restrictions which obtain in a temple, then, where only a priest can officiate, are not evident for the same deity in the home.

Although families sit together in some temples, men and women usually sit on either side of the shrine on the floor (there are no chairs). Worship can take place at any time on any day. Usually a portable fire-altar is brought into the room and worshippers gather around it, facing the shrine. Some people will sing, some will chant, while others play musical instruments. The priest begins the temple *puja* by kindling the sacred fire in which are burned small pieces of wood, camphor and liquid butter, ghee. He chants verses from the *Vedas* and then prayers for purity are offered and priest and people take water into the left hand. Then, dipping the fingers of the *right* hand into the water, they touch their ears, nose, eyes, mouth, arms, body and legs. This symbolizes purification of the individual before he or she approaches his or her God. This entire ceremony is known as *havan*, the offering of fire.

Another ceremony is *arti*, worship involving light, and is a frequent act of worship, sometimes indicative of *puja* itself. *Arti* is an offering involving love and devotion to the deity. In this ceremony, symbols of the five elements of life are used, representing fire, air, earth, ether and water. A flat tray with five lights, called an *arti* tray, is waved before the images of the deities; lights are also held in front of revered personages from other religions, perhaps Guru Nanak of Sikhism and Jesus of Christianity. At other times, *arti* is performed with a single flame of burning camphor.[4] A spot of red paste is put onto the foreheads of everyone present, including the images and portraits of the deities. The mark, known as a *tilak* or *chandlo*, is made from red powder, yellow tumeric powder or sandalwood paste. The *arti* tray is taken round by the priest, and everyone present holds their hands over the flames and then passes them over the forehead and hair. This symbolizes the receiving of divine blessing, protective grace and power. Each person then receives *prasad*, often a mixture of dried fruit, nuts and sugar crystals. This represents the gift given by the deity to the worshippers, a symbol of the deity's love for them. Fuller suggests that this in some way divinizes the recipient,[5] though since *prasad* is believed to be the leftovers of the deity it could be claimed that the subordination to, and dependency of, the recipient on the deity is the central concept: *prasad* as food leftovers (*jutha*) thus indicates subordination, not identity.

Temples need not be elaborate, nor are they necessary for worship for, as we have seen, worship is something which can take place anywhere and is particularly a home-focused practice. But temples are visited daily, albeit by different people. While the priests who tend the temples of the great Gods and Goddesses need to be of the *Brahmin* class, there are, as we have seen, a variety of castes within the *Brahmin* structure. Not all *Brahmins* would be practising priests and there are many priests who are not *Brahmins* at all, who would officiate at local shrines. Of the different priests, *pujaris* are those concerned with temple or shrine ritual and they may well be illiterate, a *panda* is a temple priest at a site of pilgrimage, while a *purohit* is a family priest or *guru*. The emphasis in *puja* is on purity, love and devotion. Purity is of the utmost importance. Shoes, for example are never worn in a temple because leather is a highly polluting material, as is the street dust which is attached to them. Menstruating women are also considered to be highly polluting and would not be allowed into the temple. And while Gandhi fought hard for the rights of *dalits* to enter all temples, they are still only allowed in the outer areas of some of the bigger temples. But, in any case, temples in India are often caste orientated; *dalits* are likely to worship in a particular local temple, even frequented by certain *dalit* castes and not others and with their own *dalit* priest to officiate. Purity is also reflected in the products used in ritual. Cow products such as milk, dung and ghee are specifically purifying as well as water from a sacred river such as the Ganges. Turmeric and sandalwood are also considered to be purifying agents while water itself absorbs pollution and takes it away.[6]

Love and devotion are the main characteristics of *puja* whether at home or at the temple. And that devotion can take the form of singing, dancing, and offerings to the deity. Offerings need not be elaborate; in the *Gita* it states:

Whoever offers to me with devotion, a leaf, a flower, fruit, water, that I accept when offered with devotion by the pure-minded. Whatever you do, whatever you eat, whatever you offer in sacrifice, whatever you give, whatever austerity you practise, . . . do that as an offering to me.[7]

Devotion is also *attention* and *care* of the deities and at a basic level they are felt to be both pleased and appeased by the attention, and therefore afford protection to their devotees. But no deity *needs* such care. Fuller aptly states:

Gods and goddesses do not actually need offerings and services, because they never are dirty, ugly, hungry, or unable to see in the dark. Hence the purpose of worship is not to satisfy nonexistent divine needs, but to honor the deities and show devotion by serving them *as if* they had such needs. By this method alone can human beings adopt a truly respectful attitude toward the deities. Such an explanation of how *puja* pleases deities is logically consistent with a relatively emphatic distinction between a deity and its image, the container of divine power, because then the deity itself is not directly touched by the offerings and services made to the image.[8]

This suggests that *puja* in the form of care and attention lavished on the images of the deities provides the kind of anthropomorphic theism necessary for the worshippers themselves but, at a deeper level, the more devotion and care that is lavished upon a deity, the more an individual is able to transcend his or her own ego, and transcending the ego, is a means to the *atman* within.

Puja at shrines

Apart from the shrines in the home and the temples, there are also numerous open-air shrines in India and other eastern Hindu cultures. These may be quite elaborate affairs and some may be tended by a priest who can often be found seated at the entrance in white robes, or, they may be simply a small heap of stones. They may be quite shabby in appearance, and indeed many temples often convey this kind of image. Shrines occur generally at auspicious places. Practically every crossroads on some Indonesian islands have shrines which are decorated daily by the women of the locality. Anyone who has driven in the chaos of traffic in parts of Indonesia where there is no 'Highway Code' at all will understand the rationale of placing shrines at crossroads where accidents most frequently occur and deities need to be propitiated to help prevent them. Some shrines are deep in caves and the symbolism here is very often connected with entering the womb of the Mother Goddess.[9] It is in the very depths of such caves that the usually untended shrine is to be found.

The paths to God

In Hinduism there is a form of worship to suit the vastly different levels of consciousness of all its adherents. There is the introspective, meditative path of intuitive knowledge of Brahman, *jnana marga*, which aims to focus on the *atman* within and fuse with the Absolute, Brahman. There is the path of *yoga* of which the West is aware through the *asanas* or postures which help to free the restrictions of body and mind. There is the path of egoless action, *karma marga*, acting in the world without becoming egoistically involved in such actions or their outcomes, and there is the path of devotion, *bhakti marga*, perhaps the most popular one in Hinduism in that the ego is transcended by pouring out devotion to a particular chosen deity.

7

Life-cycle Rites in the Hindu Family

The family

The family is of considerable importance in Hinduism. While the life of the *sannyasin* is respected, the second of the *asramas*, the householder stage of life, endorses the idea that it is one's *dharma* to marry, raise a family and provide for that family in whatever way is necessary. Family life, in this case, becomes a religious obligation. Unlike the nuclear family we are accustomed to in the West, the Hindu family is normally an extended one, though there are exceptions to this these days, in view of urban settlement. The extended family includes grandparents, parents, married brothers and their whole families, so that, if accommodation is large enough, a considerable number of people can live together in the same home. This has several advantages in terms of the welfare of the old and the young. There are no state pensions for the elderly in India and the aged therefore look to their sons for support, both physically and economically, when they themselves are no longer able to contribute to the home. Having said this, the senior male of the family continues to lead it, even in advanced old age, and the senior woman holds sway, likewise, over the female members of the family. This means that respect for the elderly in a family is the normal pattern. Then, too, children have an abundance of aunts to care for them, and a large number of cousins with whom they can grow up, being close enough to them during their lives to regard them as brothers and sisters. Women share household tasks, and men share economic responsibility for the family.

Roles are fairly well defined between the sexes in the Hindu family, the men being the providers and workers, the women responsible for the running of the home. The average woman is not expected or considered able to shoulder public or social responsibility, though they do have considerable freedom in the conducting of religious practices in the home. Like Sita in the *Ramayan*, wives are expected to be loving, faithful and loyal, and willing to share even the misfortunes of their husbands; they are expected to be perfect and to treat their husbands like gods. This is not to say that they are unable to achieve status beyond the home and the family. Indira Gandhi, for example, was twice prime minister of India before her assassination in 1984. But for the average Hindu woman, particularly in rural areas, life revolves around the family, although it is the women of the family who are mainly involved in the ceremonies which mark the rites of passage in life.

Samskaras

In Hinduism there are sixteen life-cycle rites or *samskaras*, and eleven of these are concerned with the baby and young child, marking specific stages in their development. To raise children is an important aspect of the second *asrama*, the stage of the householder, and, traditionally, the birth of a boy is more important than the birth of a girl. Indeed, prestige often comes with a large number of sons, and until a Hindu male has had at least one boy born to him, he cannot progress to the next stage of life. Moreover, he will have no son to perform the important death rites which will ensure his safe passage to a better reincarnation. Boys, too, are an economic advantage in the home, whereas girls leave the home at marriage to live with their husbands' families. The *samskaras* involved with boys, therefore, tend to be more elaborate and, while not all families follow all eleven for the young child, more rites usually occur for boys than girls. But, in any case, only *Brahmin* males are likely to undergo all of them.

Birth, like death, is seen as a time of considerable pollution and danger, when the unborn child, and particularly the newly-born child, is very vulnerable to evil forces. So the first three *samskaras* are devoted to the safety and welfare of the unborn child, while the fourth ceremony takes place at birth. At this time, the child is ritually washed and has sacred sounds whispered in its ear, while the sacred syllable *aum* is written on its tongue with honey. Probably the most popular of the early *samskaras*, however, is the naming ceremony, *namkaran*, which is held on the twelfth day after birth by the twice-born classes of Hindus only. This ceremony is important enough to be officiated by a *Brahmin*, though priests are not, generally, essential for ritual, especially amongst the lower castes. Wealthy

Hindus make much of this naming ceremony and it is important in that it brings to an end the period of pollution associated with childbirth. Sometimes, the baby may have its ears pierced at this ceremony, though strictly speaking ear-piercing is a separate *samskara*. The naming event is accompanied by much singing, especially of songs in which the baby's new name can be inserted. The baby's horoscope is also prepared at this time and will be very important later at the time of betrothal and marriage.

Because of the belief in the vulnerability of a young baby to evil forces, it is not usually taken out of doors until the third or fourth month, and this occasion itself is a *samskara*, but so that the baby does not attract the evil eye it is dressed in dark clothing for the occasion and lamp black is put on its forehead to hide its beauty. When, at about six months old, the baby is given its first solid food, a little boiled rice mixed with ghee and honey, this is the occasion for another *samskara*, as is the cutting of the child's hair for the first time, a ceremony made much of by *Brahmin* boys. For some, it is this ceremony of hair cutting which marks the end of any remaining pollution connected with the birth process.

Upanayama: the sacred-thread ceremony

Of the eleven rites, the sacred-thread ceremony is the most important. It is practised only by members of the three highest classes – *Brahmins*, *Ksatriyas* and *Vaisyas* – but today it is mainly *Brahmins* and wealthy Hindus who carry out the ceremony. Killingley, however, notes that *advija* castes have adopted their own sacred-thread ceremonies.[1] A *Brahmin* boy would be given the sacred thread at the age of six, eight or ten, a *Ksatriya* up to the age of twelve, and a *Vaisya* up to the age of fourteen. He is expected to wear it for the rest of his life and although it is changed at special times, the new one is put on before the old one is removed, so he is never without it. The thread, consisting of three strands of cotton yarn, reminds the Hindu that he is indebted to God, to his parents and to his teacher, his *guru*. But the three strands may also represent the *Trimurti* or remind the wearer of the need for disciplined mind, speech and body. The ceremony is preceded by singing, dancing and feasting during the few days before the sacred thread is placed on the boy by his *guru*; it is placed over his left shoulder and under his right arm. He is then twice born (*dvija*), born again, and has come of age. The ceremony marks the beginning of his formal education.

Betrothal and marriage

The twelfth rite is that of betrothal, prior to the thirteenth which is marriage. There is considerable variety in marriage customs, even in the same caste. Unlike birth and death, marriage is a time of great purity in contrast to pollution; the bride and groom are considered to be like deities, like Ram and Sita, Visnu and Laksmi, and are treated accordingly. Hindu weddings may last as long as six days before the wedding night, and may continue for the same length of time afterwards. These days would be taken up with singing, dancing, feasting and various religious and social rites. The wedding ceremony, itself, however, only lasts for two to four hours. Traditionally, it should take place at night, because marriage vows are unchangeable and as final as the pole star, which is only seen at night.

In India, when the child reaches marriageable age, the family searches for a suitable partner. The marriage is arranged by mutual agreement of the families and involves the satisfaction of precise practical criteria, which would take into consideration caste, horoscope, education, financial and social backgrounds. An example of an advertisement in the matrimonial column of a newspaper is the following:

> Wanted, Vadama Non-Bharadwaja (caste) bridegroom for girl 28 Servai Thosham, Secondary Grade trained, well versed in domestic duties. Also bride for her brother, 31, employed in State Bank Madurai, drawing RS 450. Mutual alliance alone considered. Reply with horoscope and full particulars Box No. 6731 c/o *The Hindu*.

Traditionally, the girl's parents search for a husband, though in low castes it is the other way round. Financial arrangements are still important, even though the dowry system is now illegal in India. Among high caste Hindus, a dowry would be expected from the girl, but in low castes, the bride is paid for.[2] There are still cases of girls being ill-treated by their new in-laws if their dowry turns out to be insufficient, or even dowry-deaths, where new brides are killed. The poorer the family, the heavier the dowry, but an educated girl, who could actually earn a living, would only need a small dowry. In many families today, expensive presents have replaced the dowry, the presents being given to an entire family by the bride's parents; the closer the relative, the more expensive the present.

Such arranged marriages are difficult for those of the Western tradition to understand, but different sociological factors need to be recognized. The woman will be brought into the male's family, often a large extended one, and will have responsibility as a mother. It is argued that this necessitates the same caste and similar cultural and religious background: a new bride will be unable to adapt to her new home if she is from a different caste. Yet there has been much debate over this aspect of arranged marriages in Hindu life. There is a certain clash of cultures for some Hindu children living, for example, in Britain. Having been born in this country, they question the old tradition. The reasons for such marriages which are applicable to the extended family are not always relevant to the situation of the nuclear family. Thus in Britain, the Hindu's situation has been slightly modified in terms of arranged marriages, for boys and girls have the ability to intermix at school more freely and sometimes socially before marriage, whereas in India they have no such opportunity. Hindu parents in Britain today will sometimes accept their children's wishes provided they see that the marriages are suitable according to the criteria of educational and social background. In this case the marriage may be said to be semi-arranged. Child marriages are now forbidden by Indian law though they still occasionally occur. Such a practice used to be a means of ensuring that illicit sexual relations – and hence mixed-caste relationships – could never take place. The practice, though virtually obsolete, highlights the importance of caste purity in India.

Vivah: the marriage ceremony

Marriage is the domestic obligation of the twice-born or high classes in Hinduism. It is regarded as a religious duty for the production of sons and the stability of family and societal life. The marriage ceremony as a religious rite is very important. It is solemn, profound, and complex in form, stressing the mutual co-operation of bride and groom and, in many ways, is the combining of two *families* as much as two individuals.

Before the wedding takes place there are traditional customs to be observed which vary enormously. Anointing the prospective bride and groom with oil and turmeric usually takes place several times on the days running up to the actual ceremony. In particular, the family deities would be invoked, and Ganesh, the deity of Good Fortune, who removes all obstacles, would be a prominent focus of *puja*. The wedding ceremony is conducted within a specially erected canopy, called a *mandap* or *mandva*, which is decorated with coloured lights and tinsel. It is set up at the home of the bride, for it is the bride's family who will pay for the wedding. Before the wedding ceremony, the bride is ritually bathed, and the hands and soles of the feet are decorated with henna dye, making very attractive, intricate and long-lasting *mehndi* patterns. For the wedding, the bride generally wears a red sari threaded with gold and an immense amount of traditional jewellery, particularly on the head and face. It is traditional too for the bride to look particularly sad at her wedding and she is usually helped by her sisters as she walks to take her place under the canopy with her husband to be.

The bride's parents welcome the bridegroom's family ceremonially and both sets of relatives attend the ceremony performed by the priest. The father of the bride welcomes the bridegroom in a reverential, worshipful manner in view of the Hindu belief of Brahman within all and on this day the groom is treated as a god, the bride as a goddess. The father uses the same gestures as in *puja* before a deity; the groom's feet are washed and he is given the best of offerings. Traditionally, the groom should travel to the bride's home on a horse, with much ceremony and parading, so in India, he would have travelled at least some of the way in this manner before being greeted at the bride's home.

During the ceremony, the genealogies of the bride and groom are recited. A sacred fire is lit and offerings are made while *mantras* from the *Vedas* are recited. The ceremony is a few hours long but the most important part is the circumambulation of the sacred fire: it is this action, called *phera* or *bhavar*, which seals the marriage. On the last circumambulation, the bride, who has been seated on the right of the platform with her family, now sits on the left, with her new in-laws; she has effectively passed from one family into another. While customs vary, there is usually some form of binding the couple together symbolically. A white cord may be strung between the shoulders of the couple, representing the indissolubility of their new bond in marriage, or, threads are tied round each others' wrists. Another important feature is the sacred ceremony of seven steps, *saptapadi*, in which the couple take seven steps, each one symbolizing a different aspect of, and wish for, the couple's future life together – food, strength, increasing wealth, good fortune, children, long life and eternal friendship. These seven steps are the blessings hoped for in the marriage. At the close of each round, the bride touches a stone symbolic of the rock-like stability given to herself, to her husband, and to his family, and the ability to overcome obstacles throughout married life.

There is much emphasis on the unity of the two and the wish for a happy and long life for them both. The groom promises to be moderate in *dharma*, *artha*, and *kama* (what is right, material wealth, and pleasure), to care for his wife, allow her financial management of the home and to be faithful and affectionate to her. The bride promises support to her husband, to be faithful, non-extravagant, and to render her wifely duties without expecting anything in return. She promises to respect her husband's family and friends – an important consideration in view of her taking up home with her new in-laws – and to perform her domestic chores well. The ceremony concludes with prayers for good fortune and peace. It is generally followed by great celebration, often of lavish expense, the result of years of saving by the family.[3] The ceremony usually takes place in the home, but it may be followed by a visit to the temple. According to tradition the couple are to be continent for the first three days; this is an indication of the importance of the *contract* in the marriage. A ceremony known as *gauna* marks the departure of the bride to the home of the groom, but in the case of child marriages which, though illegal, still occur in India, the girl will stay at her parents' home until puberty.

Life in the home

It is the women of the family who are responsible for the running of the home and the raising of children. Motherhood is regarded as very important and a woman is considered to be a failure if she is without children, especially if she has no son. Death in childbirth is particularly appalling to the Hindu mind. It is the women, especially the head woman of the family, who perform *puja* in the home, but no menstruating woman is allowed near the deities of the home shrine because, during menses, a woman is highly polluted, and purity in *puja* and *darsan* is, of course, essential. Additionally, a menstruating woman will not be able to enter the kitchen or come into contact in any way with food preparation. Neither can she enter a temple or shrine outside the home. Only after ritual bathing at the end of menses can a woman then resume normal domestic and religious life in the home. High caste women tend to be subject to more seclusion than lower caste women during menstruation. The status of wifehood and motherhood is ideal in the Indian mind and a married woman is considered 'auspicious' because of her status.[4] While controlled by their husbands, married women generally support the idea of this auspicious but subordinate status.

Despite the emphasis on motherhood, abortion, which is legal in India, is very frequent. The amniocentesis test is now used widely to ascertain the sex of a child, and if the outcome suggests that the foetus is a girl, it will often be aborted. Abortion, then, has become a means of birth control for many Hindu women. Particularly amongst the poor, it is better to abort in the case of a girl than to support another child and in any case, the dowry price is so high for a low caste girl that it is cheaper to abort.[5] While contraception is praised and encouraged by the Indian government the importance of having sons to provide economic support, particularly in old age, and the need for sons to perform death rites, means that contraception is unlikely to be used until sufficient sons have been born. The Indian government has been sufficiently concerned about the misuse of the amniocentesis test to restrict its use to determine sex in 1994.

Whatever life in the home may be like, divorce for a woman is difficult, and practically impossible for women of the higher castes, despite the fact that the Hindu Marriage Act of 1955 made divorce legal for women. While Babb suggests that divorce is quite common among the lower castes[6] as is also the remarriage of widows, there is still a general feeling in village life that a wife is to blame if her husband dies. The divorced woman is regarded as 'inauspicious' without her husband, and like the widow she can become something of an outcaste. However, particularly in urban areas, women do have more status these days than hitherto and can now own land, have their own salaries and open bank accounts. Yet a woman's self esteem still has much to do with devotion and loyalty to her husband. Customarily, without a husband, a woman is too inauspicious to attend weddings, to wear jewellery or coloured saris, and should cut her hair as a mark of her inauspicious nature. It is something of a sin if a woman survives her husband. And while such harsh ideas are in decline, they have by no means disappeared, particularly among the higher castes.

Death

Death is the last *samskara* and there is far more emphasis in death rites on the deceased joining his or her ancestors than the more philosophical ideas of *samsara* and *moksa*. Like birth, death is considered to be a highly polluting time, so polluting in fact that the deities of the home are often removed entirely, and no one would partake of food from the home of the deceased. Contact with the dead cuts a person off from the normal routine of life. It is the sons of a person who become so important in the rites of passage concerning death. Their role is to send the spirit of the deceased to the realm of the ancestors through correct ritual. Immediately afer death, the deceased becomes a *preta*, a 'ghost' and, if not sent on its way correctly, will disturb the living by remaining with them and causing them harm. The death rites are designed to change the *preta* into a *pitri*, an 'ancestral spirit': this takes twelve days in all and when this is done, the spirit of the deceased leaves the family for the abode of his or her ancestors. On the twelfth day, four balls of rice, called *pinda*, are prepared to symbolize the union of the deceased with his or her forebears: one rice ball is for the newly deceased, three for the preceding three generations. The special ceremonies which are performed during the twelve days following the cremation are known as *sraddha* ceremonies. Death rites are important not only for the future of the dead but also for the continued welfare of the living and, since only a male can effectuate them, the importance of sons to ensure the safety of the deceased spirit is emphasized.

Cremation has always been the traditional Indian means of disposing of human remains. The reduction of the body to ashes by fire is not only an extremely hygienic way of disposing of the dead in the heat of India (fire being an efficient purifier) but cremation is commensurate with the Hindu belief that the soul is immortal but the body not so. The deceased is washed, and the corpse is wrapped in a cloth, white for men and red for women, and carried to the cremation ground in a procession led by the eldest son, who also lights the funeral pyre. The dead body will be placed on the funeral pyre with the feet facing south towards the home of Yama, ruler of the dead. It is covered with wood, and then ghee, and funeral rites are enacted by a priest. After cremation the youngest member of the family leads the procession home. The bones of the cremated body are thrown into water, an important process because immersing something in water has a cooling and purifying effect and, in this case, is deemed to purify and release the spirit from this world. The cremation grounds are to be found on the banks of a river for the purpose of immersing the bones in such a way. A Hindu funeral is an inauspicious occasion: refreshment will not be partaken of by the mourners since the life-giving process should have no association with death and any food would carry pollution.

While cremation is the desired method of disposal of the dead, burial is not uncommon. The lower castes in particular practise burial because it is cheaper, and children who die are buried rather than cremated, especially babies who die before the naming ceremony. A *sannyasin* will also not undergo cremation. Cremation frees the soul from the body, but because it is believed that a *sannyasin's* soul is already at one with Brahman, the body is dropped into the river and weighted with stones.

As it sinks, disciples chant hymns and blow conch shells to celebrate the union of the soul with God. Some, however, are buried, for they have abandoned their families and sons and have given up all identity to make death rites pertinent to them as individuals. *Gurus* may also be buried, often seated in the lotus position. A monument called a *samadhi* is used to mark such a place of burial.

In the towns of India, cremation by gas or electricity is the norm as it is in Britain. In Britain the custom is slightly different because of legal requirements. The body will be washed and dressed in new clothes, placed in a coffin and surrounded by flowers. Cremation has to take place after a few days because of the necessary legal arrangements. At the crematorium the priest will talk about the life of the person and after returning to the house, prayers are said for the departed soul in front of the sacred fire. The ashes of the deceased would preferably be sent to a relative in India to be scattered in the Ganges or, failing this, cast into a fast-flowing river in Britain.

When the period of death rites is over, the close, male relatives cut or shave their hair in order to remove the pollution of death. The house has to be thoroughly cleaned and a washerman is given all the linen to wash, the washerman being traditionally low caste, because polluted materials are continually handled. Only when the house has been thoroughly cleansed can the household deities be returned.

8

Symbols

Aum

Hinduism is replete with symbols. They serve the purpose of projecting the mind beyond the immediate to what is less expressible, very often an abstract, metaphysical concept. From the opposite perspective, symbols make absolutes more tangible in conception and more easily understood. The symbol most sacred to Hindus is *Aum* or *Om*, which represents Brahman, the vastness of the cosmos and its oneness. It is made up of three Sanskrit letters, *aa*, *au* and *ma* which, when combined together, make the sound *Aum*.

The symbol represents both the unmanifest (*nirguna*) and manifest (*saguna*) aspects of Brahman and so is, in itself, a *saguna* means of knowing the Unmanifest Brahman.

Aum is the one eternal syllable of which all that exists is but the development. The past, the present, and the future are all included in this one sound, and all that exists beyond the three forms of time is also implied in it.[1]

Aum is thus believed to be the basic sound of the world and to contain all other sounds. But while it symbolizes the most profound concepts of Hindu belief, it is written daily, at the head of letters, at the beginning of examination papers, for example. At a deeper level it is also used as a *mantra* when, if repeated with the correct intonation, it can resonate throughout the body so that the sound penetrates to the centre of one's being. Then, since *Aum*, Brahman, is the very essence of the self, the *atman* is able to be experienced. All possibilities and potentialities exist in *Aum*; it is everything that was, is, or can yet be. Even though it is *everything*, as ultimately it is the nature of Brahman, it cannot be defined in any way. Since *Aum* expresses so much and symbolizes what is spiritually perfect, the symbol is worn as a pendant by many Hindus and will be found on posters or in some form on family shrines, as well as in temples.

The *svastika*

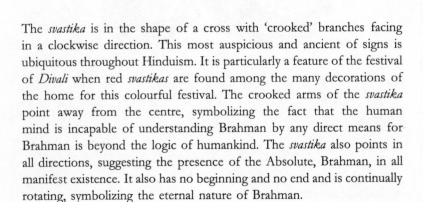

The *svastika* is in the shape of a cross with 'crooked' branches facing in a clockwise direction. This most auspicious and ancient of signs is ubiquitous throughout Hinduism. It is particularly a feature of the festival of *Divali* when red *svastikas* are found among the many decorations of the home for this colourful festival. The crooked arms of the *svastika* point away from the centre, symbolizing the fact that the human mind is incapable of understanding Brahman by any direct means for Brahman is beyond the logic of humankind. The *svastika* also points in all directions, suggesting the presence of the Absolute, Brahman, in all manifest existence. It also has no beginning and no end and is continually rotating, symbolizing the eternal nature of Brahman.

The lotus

The lotus is an exquisitely beautiful flower which grows in the East in the muddiest of waters. It has become a symbol of the human being living in the muddied waters of the world and yet whose soul can rise and blossom, like the lotus flower, to the point of enlightenment. The flower is symbolic of the true soul of each individual. The well-known meditation position, the lotus posture, is based on the flower. The flat green leaves of the plant are like the outspread knees when the feet are pulled up onto the opposite thighs, and the straight back is like the lotus flower itself. The lotus is also a symbol of creation. Brahma the creator God in one of the creation myths of Hinduism is said to come forth from a lotus which blooms from the navel of Visnu.[2]

Deities as symbols

All Hindu deities are themselves symbols of the inexpressible, undefinable Brahman and point towards It. Each deity, then, symbolizes a particular aspect of Brahman, for example, Visnu represents the preserving aspect; Siva the opposite, dissolving one. But each individual deity also carries many characteristics of dress which themselves are symbols of the deity's powers. The number of arms, usually four, signifies these great powers, and the objects held in the hands are also themselves symbols. Brahma, for example, holds one or more of the *Vedas* in his hands, suggesting his power over creative and religious knowledge. Visnu holds a conch which symbolizes the five elements and eternity, a discus which symbolizes the mind, a bow to symbolize causal power and a lotus which symbolizes the cosmos. The very position of the hands tells devotees that the deity is offering benevolence or tells them not to fear, or to take refuge at their feet. Once the characteristic symbols of the deity are known, then the different deities can easily be recognized. Visnu and his *avatars* are always dark in colour, symbolizing that although associated with creation and light, birth must be followed by death. Krisna can always be recognized by the peacock feather he wears in his head and by the fork-shaped mark on his forehead. It is this latter symbol by which Vaisnavites can be recognized, as any manifest form of Visnu as well as Visnu himself. Krisna often carries a flute, the symbol of the divine music which calls the soul to God. Siva, when not symbolized by the *linga*, can be recognized by the three horizontal lines on the forehead, the blue throat as a reminder of the poison he drank to save the world, the trident which represents the three *gunas*, and the whiteness of his skin which shows that although he dissolves life, what dies must also be reborn. Similarly, other deities can be recognized by the symbols associated with them.

9

Food and Dress

Vegetarianism

Although Hinduism has few dietary laws, eating habits are influenced by religious belief, by caste regulations, and particularly by concepts of purity and pollution. On a more general level, since all life is sacred, it is considered wrong to kill animals for food, though many Hindus are not vegetarians. The cow, however, is sacred to Hinduism, and few Hindus would partake of beef or veal. While cows are not exactly worshipped, they are well-loved and would not be slaughtered for meat. They can be seen roaming through the towns in India, grazing on grass verges or munching vegetables discarded by street sellers and, often, vegetables which are for sale! Bahree points out, rather well, that the cow is sometimes believed to be a symbol of the earth because it gives yet asks nothing in return.[1] Apart from being afforded protection on religious grounds, it makes good economic sense to protect the cow. Meat is difficult to preserve in the heat of India, and few people have the economic standing to afford refridgeration. It is also expensive, so even those Hindus who are not really vegetarians cannot afford to buy meat on a regular basis. Generally, too, meat is not considered to be very healthy to eat, whereas the by-products of the milk of the cow are considered to be very important for good health.

From a religious point of view, meat is a polluting material and considering that many homes have their shrines in the kitchen, the purest place in the house, bringing meat into the proximity of the deities would be sacrilegious, polluting the deities themselves. Some Hindus will not allow meat anywhere near the kitchen. On the other hand, people flock to the temples or shrines for the ritual slaughter of animals, the goat in particular, as an offering to the female deities. Since such sacrifice to the Mother Goddess, especially Kali, is such an important aspect of ritual, it is difficult to conclude that a principle such as *ahimsa*, non-violence to any living creature, is adhered to entirely. The sacrificial goat is offered to the deity, its *essence* extracted by the deity, and it is then returned to the owner as *prasad*, for cooking and consumption. *Brahmin* priests are never involved in such sacrifice which is officiated over by lower caste priests mainly in the smaller village shrines and temples. Deities, however, could never be wholly offered animal sacrifices without other forms of *puja* offerings. Hindus have come to regard those who accept animal sacrifice as belonging to inferior castes, and their deities as inferior recipients.[2]

There are a significant number of Hindus who are vegetarians and most of these would avoid eating eggs also. Since India is so vast, there are considerable regional variations in diet and cooking, but there are a number of common elements. High protein foods are particularly important in a vegetarian diet, and *dal*, a lentil dish, is popular throughout India. Rice dishes are a particular feature of Southern India, and the flat bread known as *chapatti* or *paratha* is preferred in many parts of India. Vegetables cooked in spices are also popular.

Caste regulations

A major area of influence on eating habits is that of caste. Traditionally, a Hindu should not accept food, especially cooked food, from someone of a lower caste, since the food would be polluted: any food which another person touches or smells, is really polluted, but cooked food is particularly vulnerable to the *essence* of the person cooking it. The danger of pollution is far greater from cooked than uncooked food. Though the custom is now dying out, it used to be common sense to employ only *Brahmin* cooks and waiters in a restaurant, because anyone can eat the food prepared by a *Brahmin*.

Pukka and katcha foods

Certain foods are preferred because they are *pukka*. These would be foods which are deep-fried in ghee. In contrast, leftovers which are re-heated, or left to be eaten later or the next day, are considered as stale food, *katcha*. Food cooked in water is especially *katcha*. From a religious point of view foods which are *sattvic* in quality are superior. The *Bhagavad Gita* tells us that such foods are '*savoury, fatty and substantial*'[3] by which is probably meant milk, butter and cheese. Also included would be rice, pulses, sugar and wheat. *Rajasic* food, the *Gita* says is '*bitter, sour, saline, excessively hot, pungent, dry and burning*'[4] and these are foods which are likely to make the eyes water and the stomach burn – something which could be said for the strong curries often associated with Indian food! Garlic and onions fit into this category, being harmful *rajasic* foods which militate against the more desirable *sattvic* qualities in life. *Tamasic* foods are stale, tasteless, rotten foods which have lost their goodness through staleness and over cooking. Rotten food is really something left over from one day to the next.[5] Meat would certainly be considered as a *tamasic* food. The particular balance between hot and cold foods and heating and cooling in cooking is believed to be very important for bodily and spiritual health.[6]

The role of women

It is the women of the home who are responsible for the diet being in charge of all food preparation and even of the keeping of fasts in the family. They ensure that the kitchen is kept thoroughly pure and that no impurities such as leather are worn. Visitors would not, normally be allowed in a Hindu kitchen because of such purity rules. Normally women bathe before preparing food, and it is the senior woman who organizes its preparation. Since the left hand is associated with unclean aspects of life such as use of the toilet, it is only the right hand which is used in eating food. But while women maintain the strict codes of purity in the preparation of food, they themselves eat only the leftovers from the males of the family. The *Laws of Manu* an ancient religious code which lays down all sorts of regulations for class, caste, and kingly rule, had much to say about the role of women but emphasized especially that a woman should treat her husband as a god. And since food was offered to the deities and the 'leftovers' were received back by the worshipper, the women were to treat their husbands as gods and eat their leftovers as *prasad*, a custom which is still maintained in India today, though not so frequently in Western Hindu cultures.

Dress

There is no particular type of religious dress required in Hinduism and local and regional styles differ considerably. The traditional dress for women is the *sari*, a piece of material five or six metres long which is wrapped and pleated around the waist and then drawn round over the shoulder so that the free end is left loose and flowing. In different parts of India, the *sari* is wrapped in different ways. In company, in the temple or when attending *puja*, women will normally cover their hair with the loose end of their *saris*, or they may use a separate long piece of material called a *dupatta*: this is light in weight and matches the *sari*. Covering the head is a sign of respect to God as well as to other people. Underneath the *sari*, an ankle length skirt is worn and a bolero-type blouse called a *choli*. In northern India, especially in the Punjab, women prefer to wear light, baggy trousers called *salvar*, and a long loose-fitting tunic called a *kameeze*.

Indian women in general love jewellery and are particularly fond of bracelets and anklets. Bangles, rings, necklaces, earrings, toe rings and nose rings are also popular, as well as a jewel in the nose, something which has become popular amongst Western young people today. Long earlobes have always indicated nobility in Indian tradition and were a sign of respectability. Sometimes heavy earrings are used to stretch the earlobes slightly. A married woman can be recognized by the *bindi* in the centre of the forehead, between the eyebrows. This may be applied with a spot of red paste, or it may be a circle of adhesive felt which can more easily be put on. Felt *bindis* have the advantage of being decorated with sequins and can be different shapes. In some parts of India it is fashionable for young girls also to wear a *bindi*. Dress is designed to cover the legs, but Hindu women can have their arms and midriff bare.

Hindu men very often wear Western clothing, but many will wear a *kurta-pyjama*, a loose-fitting shirt and trousers. Typical Indian village dress for men has customarily been the *dhoti*, a garment immortalized by Mahatma Gandhi. This single piece of usually white cloth is worn wrapped around the waist and tucked up between the legs. In the south of India, a *lungi* is worn by men, a piece of usually brightly coloured cloth which is also wrapped round the waist but which reaches almost down to the ankles. The wearing of a turban is usually associated with Sikh men, but in India some Hindu men will also wear turbans though they are tied in a very different way to Sikh styles.

10

Hindu Festivals

Hindu religion is rich in life, colour and emotion. Its festivals, in particular, are characterized by happiness, music, perfumed fires, countless candles, gaily decked elephants, and so on. Life is to be enjoyed, for the world is the joyous creation of God. Festivals are connected with the moon in Hinduism because the religion follows a lunar calendar. In some ways they are also suited to the seasons; the hot dry seasons will be characterized by certain types of festivals, while the rainy season, which brings out poisonous snakes, scorpions and disease, when the people feel insecure, will be reflected in different types of festivals. *Raksa Bandhan* is a good example of this.[1] Additionally, the rainy season begins about mid-June and is a time when the deities are believed to be asleep and demons and evil forces can become active. Hindus are very fond of their festivals for they are a time of great enjoyment. Most families have a festival day each week, depending upon the particular God they worship. Monday, for example is in honour of the God Siva, or the Moon, Tuesday Hanuman (also Saturday), Wednesday Ganesh, Thursday Sarasvati, Friday the minor goddesses, and Sunday the Mother Goddess. Saturday is a very inauspicious day, a 'dark' day, governed by the planet Saturn. Some festivals are celebrated every fortnight, others every year.

On a festival day a purification bath would be taken (in India, if possible, in a holy river or lake) and new, or at least clean, clothes put on. There would be longer *puja* than usual, singing, dancing, fasting, feasting and visits to the temple. Festivals can be national, regional or local celebrating also births and deaths of famous local or national people. The government even allows each citizen to have occasional days' holiday for celebration of festivals on those days when public holidays do not occur.

The Festival of Divali (Oct./Nov.)

Divali, a five-day festival, means 'cluster of lights', the name being a contraction of *Dipavali*. The festival is so called because homes, cowsheds, temples, offices, etc., are decorated with coloured electric lights or clay *Divali* lamps (*divas*) containing a wick floating in oil. Lots of stories are associated with the festival. It is said that the Goddess Kali was born at this time, and that the Goddess Laksmi, the wife of the God Visnu, visits each house which is clean and brightly lit and will bring gifts and prosperity during the coming year. Another story concerns the God Visnu in his incarnation as Krisna. Krisna defeated a demon called Naraka but when Naraka was dying he asked a boon of Krisna. Naraka asked that his death should be mourned on its anniversary but in a happy way, with new clothes, fireworks, greetings sent to family and friends and lights to brighten the night. Krisna granted his request with the festival of *Divali*. However, the most well-known story connected with the festival is that of the *Ramayan*. In the holy city of Benares, the *Ramayan* is acted out over a period of thirty days for the festival. When Ram eventually found his wife Sita, with the help of Hanuman the monkey, they eventually returned to Ayodhya, from which place they had been banished fourteen years previously. They were met with joyous celebration and rows and rows of coloured lights to mark the triumph of light over darkness, good over evil.

On *Divali*, families will try to meet together, and a man will take his wife home to her parents. Boys are often given a party by their sisters and cousins, new clothes are worn, and each house is cleaned and decorated. It is a time for whitewashing the houses and buildings and making everything look as clean and attractive as possible. Girls make intricate designs called *rangoli* patterns in coloured chalk in front of their houses. Animals are washed, groomed and decorated and will have bells put around their necks and special food to eat. The festival marks the beginning of the new business year so accounts are settled so that no one is in debt and everyone, particularly children, tries to turn over a new leaf. In Britain there would not be so much emphasis on outdoor activities, but a lot of dancing, speeches and parties. In India, dancing groups tour the towns and cities performing for money. Presents will be exchanged and *Divali* cards sent to friends and relatives at home and abroad.

Divali also has a personal touch, since each girl makes a *Divali* lamp of her own and in India if she lives near a river, she will set her light afloat on the river on a small raft. This is done in darkness, and if the lamp stays alight for as long as she can see it, she will have good luck during the coming year. The festival also chases off demons, and peals of bells are often heard to ensure this. In essence, *Divali* is representative of the triumph of light over darkness, of good over evil and the rows of *divas*, the little lamps outside the homes, are symbols of this light and goodness.

Holi (March/April)

Divali has traditionally been associated with the *Vaisya* class although every Hindu celebrates it. Similarly, *Holi* is a festival associated with the *Sudras*, the fourth class, and is celebrated in northern and central India. While not strictly a New Year festival, since the New Year begins two weeks later, many of its festivities are linked with the destruction in flames of the old and the bringing in of the new. It occurs at the time of the spring harvest and is associated with riotous merriment. Because it welcomes spring, it is an outdoor festival, although in Britain it is often celebrated in February. In Indian villages, bonfires are lit and mothers often carry their babies five times in a clockwise direction around the fire, so that Agni the god of Fire will bless the babies with a successful life. People throw coloured powder dyes over everyone they meet or use such things as bicycle pumps to squirt this coloured water over anyone they can.

Holi possibly derives its name from Holika. Holika was the daughter of the mythical King Hiranyakasipu who commanded everyone to worship him. His little son Prahlada refused to do so and even learnt his alphabet with the names of the Gods – V = Visnu, S = Siva, etc. His father ordered Holika to kill him and she, possessing the ability to walk through fire unharmed, picked up the child and walked into a fire with him. Prahlada, however, chanted the names of God and was saved. Holika perished because she did not know that her powers were only effective if she entered the fire alone. The practice of hurling cowdung into the fire and shouting obscenities at it, as if at Holika, suggests a strong association of the festival with this particular story. But others celebrate *Holi* in memory of Krisna. In the legends about Krisna as a youth he is depicted as getting up to all sorts of pranks with the *gopis* or cowgirls. One prank was to throw coloured powder all over them, so at *Holi* images of Krisna and his consort Radha are often carried through the streets. *Holi* occurs at the hottest time of the year and is characterized by 'heated' behaviour. At this festival practices are allowed which could not obtain at other times. It is obviously easy to victimize someone with whom an old score has to be settled, and there is much obscene behaviour connected with phallic themes. There is a relaxation of normal caste rules, though not to the extent that *Brahmins* and *dalits* would engage in any kind of contact, and servants do not take advantage of their masters. Yet some sources suggest that *dalits* will chase *Brahmins*, and labourers' wives have been known to beat the shins of their rich, high-caste farmers.[2] Women, especially, enjoy the freedom of relaxed rules and sometimes join in the merriment rather aggressively. It is a time too when meat can be eaten by vegetarians, a time when pollution is not important, a time for license and obscenity in place of the usual caste and societal restrictions. Coming at the hottest time of the year, it is a means for people themselves to release heat, to let off steam!

Raksa Bandhan (July/Aug.)

This festival has always been associated with the *Brahmin* class. It takes place when the rainy season has begun and has ideas of protection and security built into it. It is a time when members of the twice-born classes replace their sacred threads with new ones. In addition male Hindus may be given a bracelet of string or tinsel which they wear on their right wrist. This has its significance in another Indian myth in which the wife of the god Indra tied a magic string around the wrist of the demon Bali, adopting him as her brother so that he would not kill her husband. Sisters tie such *rakhis* on their brothers' wrists and girls on the wrists of men who are their protectors. The males are expected to reward the girls with a present, and protect them wherever they may be.

Krisna Janamastami (July/Aug.)

This celebrates the birthday of Krisna who was born at midnight.The baby Krisna is greeted with singing and dancing all night long. In the temple, sweet foods are eaten by everyone. Fasting follows in the daytime and a feast in the evening, while stories about Krisna are told, sung and danced.

Ugadi (March/April)

Divali forms the New Year Festival for some Hindus but the real New Year Festival is *Ugadi*. *Ugadi* is the real time for turning over a new leaf, and renewal and change are the hallmarks of the festival. People get up much earlier on the day of the festival in order to clean the house thoroughly and decorate it with patterns of flour or rice which is hoped will bring good luck and happiness. Then a purifying bath is taken and sweet scented oils are rubbed onto the body. New clothes are worn and the rich will often buy new clothes for the poor at this time. The sacred thread of the three twice-born classes is also renewed. Many Hindus consult astrologers to discover what will happen in the year ahead.

Ram Navami (March/April)

This is the birthday of Ram, the *avatar* of Visnu. The day is a fast day when certain usual foods cannot be eaten, but unusual delicacies are eaten instead. The reading of the *Ramayan* is particularly important at this festival.

Navaratri (or Durga Puja) (Sept./Oct.)

This is a nine-day festival, devoted to the goddess Durga. Navaratri means 'nine nights' and so celebrations take place in the evenings. People dance around the shrine of Durga and many fast, having one meal of fruit and sweet foods made with milk each day. The festival remembers the time when Ram turned to Durga for help when his wife Sita had been stolen by the demon king Ravan. The festival may once have been a harvest festival since sticks, perhaps representing sickles, are a prominent feature of the dances. Since Durga is the divine Mother, married daughters return home to their mothers. The festival is associated with the Spring and Autumnal equinoxes but the major festival has always been the Autumn event, the Spring festival being a minor occasion.

Dussehra (Sept./Oct.)

This festival occurs at the end of *Navaratri* and means 'the tenth'. It celebrates the defeat of the demon King Ravan in the story of the *Ramayan*, and the death of Ravan along with his brother and son. Huge images are often carried through the streets and then burnt. It is a festival to celebrate the triumph of good over evil, like many Hindu festivals. Also at this festival, the power of the deity departs from the statue of Durga and the *murti* is immersed in the river taking with it all unhappiness and misfortune. The friendship involved in the rescue of Sita from the hands of Ravan is also embodied in this festival and Hindus try to make up any quarrels and renew loyalties. It reminds them of the importance of God's love and protection. The festival is a special time for *puja* in the home and temple and for wives to worship their husbands, as Sita did with Ram. So in some parts of India wives wash their husbands' feet, put a *tilak* on their foreheads, put garlands around their necks, give them offerings, and bow down to them. In the north of India the festival actually overlaps with that of *Ram Lila*, 'Ram's Play', suggesting a possible convergence of festivals for both Durga and Ram.[3]

Mahasivatri (Feb./March)

Each lunar month is divided into two parts, the light part when the moon is waxing and the dark part when the moon is waning. *Mahasivatri* is celebrated on the thirteenth day of the dark part of every month. This day is sacred to Siva, the creator/destroyer God, and is thus called 'The great Night of Siva'. On this day there is a fast until 4.00 p.m. and then *puja* is offered to Siva. Afterwards no cereals or curries are eaten but sweet potatoes and cucumbers are a favourite substitute. Since the festival celebrates Siva's marriage to Parvati, married women worship Siva with requests for the welfare of their husbands and, traditionally, unmarried girls who keep vigil throughout the night hope that a suitable husband will be found for them by Siva. The following day is one of feasting. The festival is sometimes called *Chaturdasi*, 'the fourteenth', after this feast day on the fourteenth.

Ganesh Chaturthi (Sept.)

At this festival the elephant-headed God Ganesh, God of good fortune is worshipped. Model images of the God made in clay are carried through the streets and then dropped in the sea or lake, taking misfortune with them.

Days of remembrance also occur for more contemporary Hindus such as Swami Vivekananda, a modern preacher and leader who introduced the Rama-Krisna movement in America. The birthday of Sri Ramakrishna, the nineteenth-century saint and reformer, is also celebrated in March.

11

Yatra: Pilgrimage

The importance of pilgrimage

Pilgrimages are rituals which are *kamya*, that is to say, they are desirable but not obligatory. Because Brahman is believed to be manifest in everything, it is everywhere and so every place is sacred – rivers, mountains, coasts, groves, etc. But there are many sites where the divine has in some way become more explicitly manifest on earth and such places are subsequently felt to be the best and most auspicious sites for contact with the divine. *Yatra* to such sites is considered very auspicious and *karmically* rewarding. Consequently, everyone seems to be on the move in India. Many pilgrimages are undertaken to acquire good *karma*, to perform certain rituals for deceased ancestors (something often considered obligatory) or because of a festival. Some people make the journey through an organized tour, some by public transport and some on foot. The emphasis is very much on showing devotion to the divine, and men and women of all castes travel on the same roads to a centre of pilgrimage. Whatever caste a Hindu belongs to, visiting a sacred place is believed to purify the inner self and so bring the individual closer to God. Thus in some cases pilgrimages offset the usual caste barriers, but in others, such divisions persist, especially where commensality is concerned.

There are hundreds of places of pilgrimage all over India but twenty-four temples have become the most important. Most Hindus hope to visit the four famous shrines of the Jagannath temple at Puri on the Bay of Bengal in East India, the temple of Ramesvaram in the South of India, Dvarkadheesh on the Western coast, and Badrinath in the north, 10,400 feet up in the Himalayas. Some Hindus spend their life's savings visiting these shrines, and will often undergo severe hardships on these journeys. At a deeper level pilgrimage, and its often arduous accomplishment, is like a journey within one's own self, a journey to the divine. The individual has to overcome both mental and physical challenges as well as plain discomfort, uncomfortable surroundings, theft, inadequate sanitation, shortage of food and so on. Such problems have to be transcended rather like the *sannyasin* transcends the world: it is a taste of the life of the renouncer. This again is an expression of devotion to God and to spiritual matters rather than material ones. Essentially, the *whole journey* becomes an act of devotion and is as important as the final destination. Pilgrims can often be heard singing *bhajans* on their way as they travel by walking or by coach. The journey itself serves to help people transcend normal ties and routines in life. Pilgrimage also helps the Hindu to be tolerant and aware of other Hindus in the vastness of India, since India has Hindus of different ethnic origins. On a pilgrimage Hindus will meet other Hindus who have differences in language and dialect and who eat different food. While undertaking a pilgrimage of a considerable distance from their homes they will encounter cultural differences as much in their own country as others travelling to different countries: India is vast enough for this to be the case. So wherever one is in India one sees Indians from all backgrounds and areas.

Benares (Varanasi)

Benares is the most famous centre of pilgrimage. It is situated on the left bank of the Ganges, at the point near where the tributary of the Ganges, the Yamuna or Varuna, joins it. Confluences of rivers are considered to be particularly auspicious sites for temples and have traditionally been associated with *asrams*, the homes of famous Hindu sages. Benares is especially associated with the God Siva who is believed to have lived there as an ascetic. Also at Benares, the thirty-day enactment of the *Ramayan* takes place each year at the Dussehra/Dasera festival. Benares is associated with Vedic and Sanskrit scholarship so Indian scholars travel there. The place is considered to be so sacred that if one dies there and has one's ashes thrown into the Ganges, purification and release from *samsara* is achieved. The same is believed of the river at Hardvar in northern India.

Puri

At Puri in Eastern India, there is a very famous temple dedicated to

Jagganath, the Lord of the Universe. Jagganath is the manifestation of the God Visnu as Master of the Universe, and pilgrims and the people of Puri pull a huge cart around the town on which a statue of Krisna is placed (this is the origin of the English word 'juggernaut').

Vrindaban and Ramesvaram

Two places in particular are associated with *avatars* of Visnu. Vrindaban on the river Yamuna is said to be the birthplace of Krisna. The area is associated with stories about the childhood and youth of Krisna and, in addition, pilgrims can visit Dvarka on the west coast, which is the place where Krisna had his palace. Also associated with the God Siva, Ramesvaram, on the southern-most tip of India, opposite Sri Lanka, is a famous place of pilgrimage associated with Ram. When Ram succeeded in rescuing his wife from the demon king Ravan he landed at this city and built a shrine to Siva in order to purify himself and his wife Sita after the killing of Ravan's soldiers.

Kumbha Mela

Every twelve years at Allahabad, and in turn at other highly sacred places, a huge religious fair is held called *Kumbha Mela*. Fifteen million people attended the last one there in January 1989. *Kumbha* means 'Aquarius' and the gatherings take place when the sun passes the sign of Aquarius and so are called *Kumbha Melas*. Literally millions of people attend these huge fairs. Such fairs, *melas*, are common and have all the characteristics of fairs with the carnival atmosphere, side shows, numerous stalls, acrobats and so on, but the *Kumbha Mela* is a spectacular event, attended by people from all over India.

Rivers

Rivers are a prominent feature of pilgrimage. Water means life, and rivers represent the life-giving nature of God. Water not only washes outwardly but is symbolic of inner spiritual cleansing. The banks of rivers have been the favourite dwelling places of the Gods, the Hindu *gurus* and sages, and have been the scene in which many Hindu scriptures have been composed. The Ganges is the most sacred river and is a gift from heaven, and to bathe in it or drink from it is highly purifying. So all

Hindus hope to bathe in the Ganges once in their lifetime and hope that their ashes will be cast into it. The Yamuna, or Varuna, is the second most sacred river and Krisna is said to have lived on its banks during his early years. Other sacred rivers are the Godavari, Narmada, Sindhu (or Indus) and Kaveri.

Hinduism is thus a complexity of widely different practices, beliefs, customs and traditions. Its classic accommodation of ideas, rather than the discarding of the old or the assimmilation of the new, has served to make it a religion of colourful and profound variety, rich in myth and containing the kind of breadth in its dimensions to cater for all levels of consciousness. Yet, despite such openness to the infinite paths to God, societal life, as we have seen, remains largely class and caste bound, so it would be true to say that while the paths to the divine are infinite, the *karmic* and *dharmic* placements of birth dictate to a considerable extent which of the multitude of paths an individual must take. This typifies the complexities of the religion rather well, illustrating the dualities and opposites which manifest existence necessarily contains – yet all are ultimately united in the Absolute, Brahman.

Part Two

History and Tradition

12

The Indus Valley Civilization

Early settlements

Somewhere during the Second Interglacial Period (400,000–200,000 BCE) *homo sapiens* appeared in India. This was the period of the Stone Age. The earliest remains of settled existence in India date to the end of the fourth millennium. It took the form of small village settlements, sufficiently independent of each other to produce different types of pottery, and to dispose of the dead differently – some by burial, some by cremation, and some by partial cremation followed by burial. This suggests that from an early date a variety of cultures obtained. Evolution has been slow in the Indian continent and remarkably long. Change is often barely perceptible even in the late twentieth century, but even in the past an urban civilization could exist which hardly changed in hundreds of years.

The Indus valley excavations

Until the early part of the twentieth century scholars believed that the Aryan invaders were the first people to bring any kind of civilization to the Indian continent. Although they brought with them no evidence of writing, when their major sacred text, the *Rg Veda*, eventually came to be written down, it gave graphic descriptions of a very barbaric invaded people – dark-skinned, flat-nosed, ugly and irreligious. Then, in the 1920s major archeological excavations in the Indus valley area revealed the remains of a quite incredible ancient urban civilization – something to rival those of both Babylon and Egypt. Indeed, it covered an area larger than Egypt or Mesopotamia, its cities scattered over almost half a million square miles. A number of cities have been excavated, but the major two are Mohenjo-daro on the west bank of the Indus, and Harappa, about

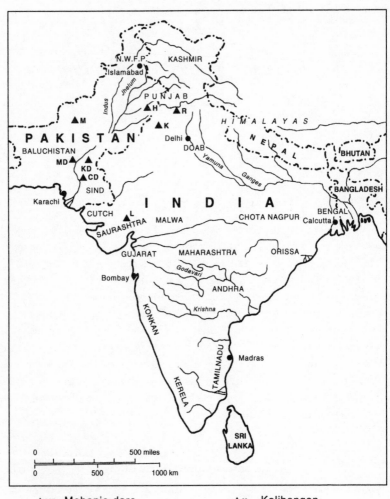

▲MD Mohenjo-daro	▲K Kalibangan
▲H Harappa	▲KD Kot Diji
▲CD Chanho-daro	▲L Lothal
▲M Mehrgarh	▲R Rupar

Map of India showing some of the major sites of the Indus Valley

250 miles further north in the Punjab. Other major cities such as Kot Diji, Kalibangan, Rupar, Mehrgarh, Chanhu-daro and Lothal have been excavated, but Mohenjo-daro and Harappa are sufficiently pre-eminent for some to suggest that they were the two capitals of the civilization. Indeed the whole area is frequently referred to as the Harappan civilization.

Excavations showed the Indus valley civilization to be a Bronze Age culture which is dated fairly consistently to about 2500–1800 or 1500 BCE. But there is a possibility of an earlier date, perhaps as early as 3300 or 3000 BCE. Today, the lowest levels of Mohenjo-daro are well below the level of the Indus, making excavation impossible: the earliest levels of urban settlement there, cannot be ascertained. We know that extensive trade took place with Sumer, Egypt and Crete. In particular cotton was exported, and the Harappan civilization must have been the earliest producers of cotton in history. Excavations at Lothal in present-day Gujarat near the Gulf of Cambay have revealed a well-built dockyard. Far from being barbarous people as portrayed by the Aryans, the inhabitants of the Indus valley lived in a highly advanced urban culture, in a sophisticated society with a wealthy middle-class and a centralized government.

The Indus valley script

Knowledge of the religion of the Indus valley culture has to remain conjectural. This is because, while there is evidence of writing from the thousands of seals which have been found, the Indus valley script defies understanding. Since the only evidence of writing comes from the inscriptions on these tiny seals about two or four centimetres square, it is very difficult to combine such inscriptions in a way which would present a coherent pattern of language. Many consider the script to be unrelated to any known language; others see it as the common substratum of Indian languages, the so-called Proto-Dravidian. Since the script has about 400 characters it cannot be alphabetic and is more likely to be syllabic, or, most probably, logographic, that is to say each character indicates a whole word – the first stage of writing in most cultures. It is written in *boustrophedon*, that is to say it is read from right to left and then left to right. The fact that this script is difficult to decipher means that there is no way in which the more abstract ideas about the religion of the Harappan culture can be ascertained. And this is something which must be borne in mind constantly in examining this period. The only evidence which obtains to give any indication of religious beliefs of the culture are the archeological artefacts – seals, figurines, masks and the structural remains of edifices, to name some. Such physical evidence is open to a variety of interpretations, and while much can be inferred in relation to the subsequent Hindu tradition, over-identification between the early and later cultures should be cautionary.

The Indus valley people

Who were the inhabitants of this sophisticated culture? Skeletal remains suggest that they were a mixture of peoples. Human remains at Mohenjo-daro revealed four ethnic types – Mediterraneans, Alpines from western Asia, Mongoloids from eastern Asia and Proto-Australoids. It is this last group which is of special interest, for some consider that it was the basic element of the Harappan culture[1] and identify it with the earliest Dravidians or Proto-Dravidians, who possibly formed the original indigenous substratum of the Indian population. Hardy, for example, suggests a pan-Indian Dravidian presence.[2] However this is unlikely, the evidence of mixed stock having more support. Some even suggest that the Mediterranean strand was the basic element of the population.[3] It is uncertain who the Dravidians were, particularly whether they were indigenous to India or immigrants from elsewhere, or even mixed stock themselves. In Baluchistan there is still an area where Dravidian speech, known here as Brahui, obtains, and Dravidian languages have survived in southern India where there are also similarities between current religious practices and the proposed religion of the Indus valley.[4] There are some suggestions, for example, that the earliest Dravidians as agriculturalists, worshipped the Mother Goddess, emphasized fertility and engaged in animal sacrifice.[5] But it would be an oversimplification to suggest that the Dravidians of the south of India are the descendants of Indus valley people who had been driven south for various reasons. All that can safely be said is that it is likely that Proto-Dravidians formed one element of the Indus valley culture and that their origin is obscure.

The Indus valley cities

The excavated cities of the Harappan culture have revealed a high level of urban sophistication. The cities were designed on a grid system, like many modern American cities. The streets ranged from wide thoroughfares of about 34 feet to smaller ones about 9 feet wide. There were many public wells and many houses had their own water source. Evidence of street lighting has also been found at Mohenjo-daro. The cities had highly efficient sewage disposal systems below the surface of the roads and there were even inspection points, making the whole sewage system the most efficient in the ancient world until the time of the Romans.[6] The houses were well structured with thick windowless walls lining the streets, the poorer having at least two rooms while the larger and wealthier as many as thirty. Staircases led to upper storeys and to the flat roofs. The houses even had rubbish chutes for the disposal of waste. All the edifices were constructed with kiln-burnt bricks – an expensive and somewhat rare building commodity in the ancient world.

The main cities incorporated separate, mounted citadels. These contained larger, more impressive and probably therefore more important buildings, perhaps of administrative or religious importance. At Mohenjo-daro stone sculptures were found in the citadel area which may have had some connection with the religious practices of the city[7] but this is a good example of how absence of written evidence makes such a suggestion suspect. At the citadel at Harappa a series of pits have been excavated containing ash, charcoal and animal bones, as well as constructions which have been suggested as fire-altars.[8] At Lothal no citadel has been found though there is evidence of a raised platform on which some of the important buildings have been located. Similar high-raised platforms have been found at the citadel site at Kalibangan and there is evidence suggestive of altars, as well as bathing places. The evidence here at Kalibangan seems more reasonably indicative of a temple or cultic area and in some of the houses at this site fire altars, separate from domestic fires, have been discovered, indicating home shrines. Stepped mounds, rather like the Babylonian ziggurats, have also been found at other excavated Indus valley sites[9] but to date, no *conclusive* evidence for temples is available. Perhaps temples were not needed and worship may have taken place in open spaces.

The great bath

The most impressive edifice at Mohenjo-daro was the 'great bath', as it has been called. This was 39 feet long, 23 feet wide and 8 feet deep. It was hardly a public bath since the houses of the main city had their own bathing facilities, so excavators have been keen to suggest some connection of it to the religious cult. It is surrounded by larger buildings and also much smaller rooms but there is no evidence to suggest that any of these were used as temple structures. A terracotta mask of a horned being and distinctive head-dresses excavated in the vicinity have led some to suggest that the whole area was one devoted to religious practices, the 'great bath' being the site of ritual purification before worship of a horned deity. Given the emphasis on ritual purification in water in subsequent Hindu practice, it is an attractive speculation but there is no written evidence to support such an idea.

Seals

Since they were great traders the Indus valley people made extensive use of small, usually square seals. These were mostly made of steatite, but sometimes of ivory and pottery, which could be carried or worn by a person, and were also used as amulets. Over 2000 of them have been found, most of them at Mohenjo-daro. They are an important discovery in that the scenes which are portrayed on them give a rich picture of aspects of life in Harappan culture, especially religious practices. Thus, where there is an absence of understanding of the Indus valley script, there is a pictorial body of evidence in the form of the seals. And on a number of seals it seems that scenes of religious significance are portrayed – prostrated people before some divine object, for example.

The most prolific representations on the seals are animals, and these are vividly portrayed – cattle, crocodiles, tigers, rhinoceros, snakes and buffalo, for example. In one scene people are depicted as prostrated before a buffalo and this must surely indicate some kind of worship. Animals seem to have been venerated for their sexuality, fertility and physical powers. Horns particularly seem to portray power. Some of the human figures appear to be divine in some way, perhaps by their central or raised position, or their particular appearance such as having elaborate head-dresses. And some seals seem to portray whole scenes of ritual pactice.

Proto-Siva

Of particular importance are three seals depicting what appears to be some kind of divine being who is seated identically on the three seals, with legs drawn up so that the knees are outspread and the heels are brought together. This is not, as so many writers like to claim, the identical posture of the great Hindu ascetic God, Siva. Nor is it the traditional lotus posture of eastern culture, where the feet are drawn up on top of the opposite thigh.[10] All that can be said of this seated figure on the seals is that the posture is a still one, a motionless one, and is a yogic one, and it is this which creates the resemblance to the ascetic nature of the Hindu God Siva. Other similarities of this figure to the later deity Siva are usually highlighted. His body is naked with the exception of his bangle-clad arms which are stretched out in front of him so that his hands rest on his knees. On two seals, the figure is possibly ithyphallic, suggesting a focus on fertility. On the largest of the three seals the figure is surrounded by wild animals, reminiscent of the later God Siva in his role as Pasupati 'Lord of the Creatures', though Siva as Pasupati is connected with domesticated animals.[11]

Cone-shaped objects have been found all over the Indus valley which scholars have identified as *lingas* – the phallic symbols associated with the God Siva, though none can be directly associated with the deity on the three seals. The original excavator of Mohenjo-daro, John Marshall, believed that the figure on one of the seals had three faces; and indeed, the God Siva is sometimes depicted so.

Thus, there are a number of possible indications that the figure on three of the seals is a forerunner of the Hindu deity Siva: he is therefore appropriately named Proto-Siva. Yet we should be cautious about pressing this identity too far. The figures on the seals are not identical and there is no reason why they should not be *different* deities: one, indeed, may possibly be female.[12] On one of the seals, the figure is presented with an elaborate horned head-dress with what seems to be a plant issuing forth from the space between the horns. There is clearly an emphasis on animal features and it is possible that at least one figure is animal faced, possibly a buffalo, and not masked, as many claim. This would accord well with the scenes of half-human, half-animal creatures portrayed on other seals. As for John Marshall's three faces, this is far from clear, the 'faces' being no more than very small protuberances or 'buds' which could indicate something very different. In fact, Alf Hiltebeitel suggests that *it takes an act of will* to concur with such a hypothesis.[13] What can be stated with more clarity is that the figure(s) on the seals was probably some kind of deity since on one seal he is flanked by kneeling attendants and two rearing cobras, one on each side. This clearly suggests ritualistic practice but, while now widely referred to as Proto-Siva, the link with Hindu Siva might be viewed with more caution.

Other seals

Some seals suggest that plants and trees were venerated. Such seals include nude figures with flowing hair. On one seal a person is depicted as kneeling at the base of a tree with a huge goat towering above him or her, while another seal shows something being placed at the foot of a tree, perhaps an offering. A 'recurrent theme', to use the Allchins' term,[14] is some sort of tree-spirit, surrounded by the branches of what seem to be pipal trees. Such beings are sometimes horned and of indeterminable sex, but the manner in which worshippers are arranged around the base of the tree, often with a certain uniformity, is suggestive of ritual practice. Clearly, a horned worshipper kneeling before a being in a tree is indicative of cultic ritual. Some authors see evidence of early *bhakti* here in view of the scenes of devotion on the seals,[15] but this is stretching the evidence too far: a distinction needs to be made between *bhakti* – the kind of loving-devotion which is a reciprocal two-way devotion between devotee and deity – and simple propitiatory devotion which is all the seals can indicate. Many seals have pictures of half-human, half-animal forms which are suggestive of divine creatures. Bulls feature considerably on seals and many writers note the connection between Siva's association with the bull Nandi (who is his mount as well as the guardian of his shrines and temples), and suggest a similar connection between Proto-Siva and the proliferation of bulls on the Indus valley seals. But there is nothing to connect the latter two directly: even the horned head-dress which adorns the figure of Proto-Siva is most likely indicative of buffalo horns and not bulls' horns, and the whole figure could even be a humanized buffalo.[16] Yet bulls certainly seem to have been part of religious practice. For example, a bull on one seal is garlanded, while on another seal a bull stands before what has been described as a 'sacred manger', which seems to be a cultic object of some sort.

From the evidence of the seals alone, then, it could be claimed that the Harappan people venerated animals and trees, tree-spirits, or even a tree goddess[17] and some kind of horned, male deity which many have seen as a precursor of the Hindu God Siva. Trees, indeed, may have been used as sacred sites which would explain the lack of archeological evidence of any edifice conclusively shown to be a temple. Half-animal, half-human creatures also seem to have been part of the religious cult and some seals portray nude, male figures with matted hair. This, and the seated, still pose of the figure on the Proto-Siva seals, might suggest some kind of ascetic aspects for the Indus valley religion. Some, indeed, see the eyes of one Proto-Siva figure as fixed on the tip of his nose – the classic yogic gaze[18] – but we must remember the size of these seals and the fact that it would be difficult for any craftsman to portray such a feature on a tiny seal. Nude, bearded, male figurines in identical upright stance might also suggest an ascetic pose, similar to that of some Indian traditions today.

Figurines

An abundance of figurines has been found from the Indus valley remains, some of animals, and some of male and female human forms. At least some of the figurines uncovered in excavations may well have been no more than ornaments or children's toys. Mohenjo-daro, for example, has yielded terracotta model carts and toy animals. But some figurines clearly belonged to the cultic world of the Harappan people. Many of the male and female figurines have heads with horns or similar appendages and might well have been deities like the so-called Proto-Siva.[19] Male figurines are sometimes characterized by goat-like beards, but like the figures on the seals, it is impossible to say whether other figurines are male or female. Many are also part animal. However, male figurines are less numerous than female ones and Basham suggested that the rigidly upright male figurines all reproduced in the same stance, and with beards and coiled hair, are indicative of a single deity.[20]

A much publicized figurine is the *dancing girl* cast in bronze found at Mohenjo-daro. She is slim and naked, except for her bangled arms and a necklace. She is long limbed (the arms somewhat disproportionately so), has elaborately plaited hair – a feature of many of the female figurines from the same period – and her facial features are Australoid/Dravidian. What was she? Was she an ornament? A figure of a dancing girl? A doll? Or was she a temple dancer or a temple prostitute as many writers suggest? There is something provocative about her stance with one hand placed on her hip but we have no context in which to place her.

Worship of the Mother Goddess

More numerous than male figurines and found throughout the whole Indus valley culture were an abundance of terracotta female figurines.

While many may have been nothing at all to do with religion, the exaggerated features characteristic of so many of them suggest that a female goddess was portrayed. In view of the emphasis on fertility indicated by other aspects of the Indus valley culture, and the proliferation of pregnancy in the female figurines, many are prepared to accept the concept of a Mother Goddess as a significant characteristic of the Harappan religion. There are some suggestions that the Proto-Dravidians as agriculturalists worshipped the Mother Goddesss as part of a fertility cult[21] and other ancient Indian peoples such as the Zhob culture have yielded figurines suggestive of the same, so it would seem that the tradition of worship of the divine in female form is a very early phenomenon, sufficiently attested to assert with some justification that the Harappan civilization continued in the same kind of tradition. So many female figurines have been found that most homes must have had them and it is possible that the very popular, more crudely formed, female figurines were the deities of the home or of the lower classes, the better crafted ones being state orientated.[22]

Most of these figurines are naked, or nearly so, and have elaborate head-dresses. Excavations at Mehrgarh have been able to uncover a fairly continuous sequence in cultural change and the more elaborate the coiffure, the later the figurine. The earliest date back to the sixth or fifth millennia and are of unbaked clay and stick-like in character but, by the time of the Indus valley culture at about the mid-third millennium, the figurines had become fairly sophisticated in style with the characteristic elaborately-coiled hair styles. This kind of evidence suggests a long tradition of worship of the divine in female form, stretching well back before the time of the Indus valley civilization. Fertility was obviously an important issue in the religion of the people. One female figurine is upside down with a plant coming out of the womb – an indication of the Mother Goddess as the genetrix and source of all vegetation. The idea is reminiscent of tantric Hinduism.[23] For a culture based on agriculture a female divine principle would have been essential and reproductive energy venerated. In later Hinduism, just as Siva is associated with the symbol of male sexuality, the *linga*, so female divinity is symbolized by the *yoni*, the female sex organ. It is possible that the ring-shaped images found throughout the Indus valley sites (except at Lothal) have some connection with the *yoni* symbolism, but the connection must remain speculative.[24] The prevalence of female figurines in the home environment may suggest that worship of the Mother Goddess was something of a domestic phenomenon. Male deities, if such they were, seem, on the other hand, to have featured at all levels of culture.

Belief in afterlife

As in the pre-Indus valley period, disposal of the dead at Mohenjo-daro and Harappa was varied – complete burial; cremation and then burial of the ashes; or burial of the skeleton after the body had been exposed to the elements. Cremation seems to have been the general trend at the height of the Indus valley culture though burial was widespread. At Lothal a cemetery has been excavated in which pairs of skeletons of the opposite sex have been found interred in a single grave. This has led a number of writers to suggest that the practice of *sati*, the death of a widow at her husband's demise, was a very early one, but the evidence for this is slim, and all sorts of equally speculative theories could be put forward for the skeletal phenomena. What is important about the burials at Mohenjo-daro and Harappa, however, is the fact that the dead were often buried with daily possessions – pots, bowls, ornaments, mirrors, and also weapons. This clearly suggests belief in an afterlife of some kind.

The demise of the civilization

The famous archeologist Sir Mortimer Wheeler, one of the excavators of the Indus sites, is immortalized on film giving a graphic description of how the cities of the Indus valley were overcome by Aryan invaders from the north – people being cut down as they fled from the marauding armies of the aggressors. But it is now known that the true picture is somewhat different. While it is true to say that waves of immigrants from the north settled in the Indus valley regions somewhere around the middle of the second millennium, and eventually extended their influence to all parts of India, these Aryans, as they called themselves, arrived at a time when the Indus valley civilization had long been in decline.

What caused the demise of the Harappan culture is difficult to say; there may have been a variety of reasons and it is perhaps wrong to look for a single cause. Moreover, there may have been different causes at different sites: Mohenjo-daro and Lothal, for example, may have suffered extensive flooding. Indeed, Mohenjo-daro is now thirty-nine feet below the level of the river plain. We know that the level of the Indus rose at

Mohenjo-daro because new houses were built on top of old ones, and streets on top of streets, to nine levels. Such flooding may have been the result of geological disturbances and must surely have caused a decline in important agricultural land along the river plain. But on the other hand, there must have been a certain amount of desiccation, a gradual drying up of the land and climate. Seals and figurines show that jungle animals like the tiger and rhinoceros inhabited the area and this suggests that in ancient times there was an abundant rainfall. But today Mohenjo-daro has usually less than ten centimetres a year in rainfall, so a gradual process of desiccation is evident. And considering the deforestation which must have taken place in order to produce the kiln-fired bricks for the cities, the Indus valley people themselves must have contributed rapidly to this process.

Then, too, there is some evidence of over-population at the end of the Indus valley period. The culture must have degenerated somewhat because the houses became squashed and small, the population becoming so dense that earlier spaciousness of planning was abandoned. There was, in short, an urban breakdown, a lower grade of life, and urban pollution. Herman rather aptly states:

All of this surely made the culture ripe for flooding, invasion, and conquest, if, indeed, there was anything left to flood, invade, or conquer.[25]

But perhaps Mortimer Wheeler's words should not be entirely dismissed. The Aryans referred to the strongholds which Indra their god destroyed[26] so there are some suggestions that the Aryan invasion was not a peaceful one. The forty skeletons which were found unburied and haphazardly fallen at Mohenjo-daro were one of the main sources of evidence for Sir Mortimer Wheeler's claims for an aggressive invasion, but they do not seem to have belonged to the appropriate level of occupation to match a mid-second millennium invasion. The Aryans called the natives of the Indus valley *asuras* 'demons', *dasyus* 'robbers', *dasas* 'slaves' and *pasus* 'two-footed animals', criticizing their flat noses, thick lips and dark skins. These were probably the Proto-Dravidian strand of the Harappan culture. Other strands seemed to have incurred less criticism, but it is clear from references such as these that the settlement of the invaders was in many ways a hostile one.

So what can be concluded from the material presented here in relation to the beliefs and practices of modern Hinduism? The Aryans brought with them a very different type of culture and different religious beliefs and practices, but it would be erroneous to suppose that these replaced the earlier ones. Rarely in Hinduism are aspects of culture lost, they are simply accommodated alongside what is new. It is likely that the religious customs of the Indus valley, in particular worship of the Mother Goddess, were maintained at the village level though it would be many centuries before we have written evidence of such practices. The village economy remained one which was based on agriculture, and fertility would have been a concept which would have influenced religious practice considerably, as it does today. The emphasis on reproductivity, albeit more metaphysically conceived of in later Hinduism, probably owes its origins to the survival of such ideas in the ancient village cultures. By 1000 BCE the sage Agastya is credited with having Aryanized the indigenous population; but the converse was also true, for many of the concepts of the Indus valley people are consonant with, or similar to, later Hindu ideas, and must have survived because they were partly accommodated by the Aryans themselves: the influence was mutual. If we look for the origins of Hinduism we would have to see them in this kind of complex accommodation of ideas, but particularly emerging from the ancient Indus valley culture on the one hand and the Aryan beliefs and practices on the other.

13

The Vedic Period

The Aryan migrations

The Aryans originally came from the plains of Central Asia east of the Caspian Sea. They were one group of many Indo-Europeans who filtered out from this area over many centuries from about 2000 BCE, other groups migrating into Europe, possibly even Ireland, and to Iran. Links between the early Iranian religion of Mazdaism, the religion of Zarathushtra and the Vedic religion of the Aryans, rather suggests that those who migrated to India may have done so via ancient Iran. But the picture once given by archeologists of a forceful invasion of the Indus valley in the mid-second millennium, as we have seen, is an erroneous one: it is probable that waves of settlement took place over a long period of time, though the Aryan scripture, the *Rg Veda*, suggests that at least part of those incursions were sizable and hostile enough to facilitate the taking of the strongholds of some of the Indus valley cities – at least what remained of them.

The first settlements of these Aryans[1] were in the Punjab and from there they gradually spread southward along the Gangetic plain until they dominated the northern part of India. They called themselves *Arya*, a term meaning 'noble'. It is derived from the Sanskrit root *ru* or *ar*, terms which are connected with the earth in some way, and really meant 'agriculturalist', but the connotation 'cultivated' or 'noble' was the one which the Aryans had in mind – a nuance of meaning which served to differentiate them from the 'barbarians' they believed they had conquered. The Indo-European origins of Old Persian, Greek, Latin, German, English, Armenian and Slavic languages are evidenced in similar linguistic cognates even today: Iran and possibly Eire, for example, come from the same root as *arya*, as does the English word *arable*. The word *Aryan* is an anglicized form of the Sanskrit *Arya*.

The Aryans were a pastoral people rather than urban like the Harappans. They were not as 'civilized' as they would have us believe in their scriptures for, though they brought the Iron Age to India, they were illiterate, their scriptures being orally handed down. They built no cities, and their artistic efforts in pottery were utilitarian and mundane: under their influence, India lapsed into a village culture for a thousand years. But they considered themselves superior to the indigenous races of India particularly because they were tall, fair-skinned and had more aquiline features. As a semi-nomadic people, their social structure was patriarchal and tribal, led by the male *rajas*, the tribal chieftains who, centuries hence, were to become monarchs. They had domesticated the horse and cow – the latter being of considerable importance in their economy and prestige. As they settled in India they built houses of wood and reed – a far cry from the spacious kiln-burnt brick houses of the Harappan culture – with cattle-rearing their main occupation, although metal workers, carpenters, potters, tanners, weavers and reed-workers were employed in the villages. Their influence was considerable and in half a century the northern part of India had become culturally Aryanized.

The *Vedas*

It is the four *Vedas* – *Rg, Sama, Yajur* and *Atharva* – which give us a picture of Vedic religion but not a totally accurate picture, for when they were eventually committed to written form after a long period of oral tradition and more elaborate developments in religious practices, the composite material which resulted only partially reflected this ancient period of Hinduism. Indeed, the major text, the *Rg Veda*, as we now know it, must have contained some material which was obsolete even when the Aryans migrated to India as well as some which was adopted after their settlement. It is difficult to assign dates to any part of it though scholars normally indicate as wide a dating as 1500–900 BCE for its collection of hymns. The picture of Aryan/Vedic religion which can be gained from the texts, then, is never wholly clear.[2]

The term *Vedic* religion needs some clarification. Strictly speaking it refers to the religion outlined in the Vedic scriptures and this would include the whole of the *Upanisads*. This latter corpus of material, however, is of such a completely different nature to the earlier Vedic material that there is a tendency to treat it separately under the category of *Vedanta* – the 'end of the *Vedas*'. This Vedantic material, therefore, will be dealt with in a separate chapter. The religious practices depicted by the four *Vedas* are termed *Aryanism* or *Vedism*. This is really to distinguish this particular period of Hindu tradition from all later traditions which, though informed by Vedism, no longer practise it. The religion of this early Vedic period is also sometimes called *Brahmanism* (*Brahminism*) after the *Brahmin* priestly influence which came to dominate it. This last term, however, is less accurate since *Brahmanism* was really a development within Vedic religion and was less evident in the very early period. It was also something which extended well beyond the Vedic period, even to the present day.[3]

It is the *Rg Veda* which dominates the Aryan sacred writings: indeed, the *Sama* and *Yajur Vedas* draw much of their material from the *Rg*. The *Atharva Veda* is somewhat different. It is more overtly magical in its nature, containing incantations and spells for all sorts of aspects of life such as success in gambling, reluctant mistresses, successful economy and wealth. While it is not devoid of more philosophical aspects it is replete with demons, sorcerors, witches and goblins and possibly contains some features of pre-Harappan animism. While it would be easy to memorize incantations and spells, the hymns of the *Rg Veda* require genius feats of memory to acquire the ability to recite faultlessly its content of more than a thousand hymns. And yet the priests could do this: with the absence of writing, oral memory excels, and the hymns were handed down in exact form to each generation of priests. Even when writing – the language of Sanskrit – was widespread in India there was a reluctance to commit these sacred texts to the written word.

Vedic religion

The early hymns of the *Rg Veda* are very much concerned with nature – the sun, the dawn and the milk-giving cow, for example. Religion seems to have been mainly propitiation of the deities to ensure a good, long life followed by a life in the World of the Fathers, the Vedic Heaven. Here, Yama, the first mortal to die, was guardian and welcomed those who had led a good life and who had not offended the gods, particularly the god of the cosmic order, Varuna. Conversely, the wicked would be condemned to the 'House of Clay', the Vedic hell. It is interesting to note that, despite the development of key concepts of *karma* and *samsara* later in Hindu tradition, these Aryan ideas of heaven and hell were accommodated alongside and not simply replaced. If there was a concern for nature in Vedic religion, this did not extend to fertility in the sense of emphasizing the principle of a Mother Goddess, and the Aryans were certainly critical of the indigenous people as 'those who worship the phallus'. Their deities were mainly male, reflecting the patriarchal character of nomadic and herd-rearing people in general. This is not to say that female deities were entirely absent. In particular, there was a 'mother' of the gods, Aditi, who gave birth to a group of seven or eight gods known as the Adityas, but Aditi is not important in the *Vedas*. Usas, the goddess of dawn, was probably the most prominent, and there are a number of very beautiful hymns in which she is featured but, to quote Heesterman, female deities 'remain diffuse, lacking in profile and to a high degree interchangeable with one another'.[4] Female divinities were thus minimal, they personified aspects of nature as wives of the gods but were not goddesses in their own right. There is, however, some evidence of the female consorts of the gods being an emanation of their power and energy – *sakti* – in the early Vedic material.[5] This may prefigure the kind of conception of *sakti* which is evident in later Hinduism. And in the *Atharva Veda* female deities are much more numerous, though no goddess rises to independent status in Vedic religion.

Vedic deities

The Aryan term for God is *deva*, which means 'shining'. The gods were the 'shining ones' and they covered three main spheres or *lokas* – the sky, where the sun gods Surya and Savitr were supreme, the heavens where the popular deity Indra was supreme and the earth, dominated by Agni, the god of fire. Deities were not strictly speaking *supernatural* beings because they were linked so much with what was natural – rain, thunder, storm, fire, wind, sound etc.[6] The gods, therefore, were symbols of the fundamental powers which control and influence existence. Many, therefore, are hardly anthropomorphized, though it would be true to say that the kind of anthropomorphism which is found in most religions is found in the *Vedas* too. This is particularly so with a god like Indra, and also with Agni:

> Be easy for us to reach, like a father to his son; abide with us, Agni, for our happiness.[7]

But despite some anthropomorphism, Vedic deities, with some excep-tions, are not well depicted in terms of their personalities; it is what they personify which is important – the elemental and fundamental powers of existence, such as consciousness, speech, wind, fire and water. Of the many Vedic deities some of the most important need to be highlighted.

Agni

Agni, the Vedic god of fire (cf. English 'ignite') is addressed in nearly a third of the hymns of the *Rg Veda*. The Aryans were well aware of both the importance of fire and its destructive nature: it could be a good servant when manipulated in sacrificial rites and when contained at the domestic hearth, but when out of control it will consume and destroy. Agni was central to sacrificial ritual because it was fire which transformed the sacrificial offering into a form accessible to the gods. And it was this offering to the gods which brought about the reciprocal divine bestowal of the very things important to the people in their daily existence. Agni *guaranteed* access to the gods:

> Agni earned the prayers of the ancient sages and of those of the present, too; he will bring the gods here.
> Through Agni one may win wealth, and growth from day to day, glorious and most abounding in heroic sons.
> Agni, the sacrificial ritual that you encompass on all sides – that one goes to the gods.[8]

Thus, it is by the medium of fire that the world of humankind and the world of the divine were believed to coalesce. Like most Vedic deities Agni should not be seen as peculiar to one role, the sacrificial one; for whenever and wherever there is fire in the sense of light, heat, combustion and energy, this is the realm of Agni. Agni is the cosmic symbol of the transformation of the gross to the subtle on all levels. This is exemplified well in the process of combustion in the body when gross food is turned into subtle energy. And on a more cosmic level we have the presence of life-giving energy in the fire of the sun.

The Aryans believed Agni to be the mysterious presence in the fire-sticks which caused ignition. Indeed, the fire-sticks which lit the sacrifice were said to be his parents, though he was born three times, not only in the fire-sticks kindled by man, but also in the lightning of the storm cloud and in the sun itself. Fire is found in so many forms and Basham wisely drew an analogy of the ubiquitous nature of fire and the later tendency in Hinduism to search for a unifying principle of the many in existence – the move to monism:

> Agni, in fact, was here, there and everywhere. Was there only one Agni, or were there many Agnis? How could Agni be one and many at the same time? Questions like these are asked in the *Rg Veda*, and show the earliest signs of the tendency towards monism, which was to bear fruit in the Upaniṣads.[9]

Zaehner, too, reiterates such a thought but adds the dimensions of opposites in the character of Agni. It was to be the transcending of such opposites, such dualities in life, which would be the means of reaching the unity of Brahman in the period of the Vedanta:

> On the macrocosmic scale he surpasses all things in greatness, on the microcosmic he is the friend and kinsman of men: he is both very great and very small, very old and very young, uniting within himself the opposites in a manner that was later to become utterly characteristic of Hindu thought.[10]

This exemplifies well the complexities of Vedic deities and warns against an attempt to see them only on a this-worldly dimension. Since they symbolize the fundamental forces within the cosmos they can be perceived at a variety of levels: Agni at the hearth, for example, and Agni the life-giving force of the universe.

Soma

Soma was both a deity and a potent, hallucinogenic drink consumed by gods, priests and worshippers alike at sacrificial ceremonies. It was important enough to have the whole of the ninth *mandala* of the *Rg Veda* devoted to it. The Vedic deity Indra was especially fond of *soma* and consumed vast quantities of it in order to enhance his strength but, even though the preparation of it is detailed meticulously in the texts, we do not know what it was. It could not have been an alcoholic beverage of any kind since it could be produced quickly without fermentation, so it is likely that it was a plant of some sort. It was equated with *amrta*, the elixir of immortality which brought, not blissful unawareness, but immortal heightened consciousness:

> We have drunk Soma and become immortal; we have attained the light,
> the Gods discovered.[11]

Like Agni, in some ways Soma is at one and the same time both a god
and access to the gods, being responsible for enabling the human being
to alter his state of consciousness in order to reach the higher states of
religious experience, transcending the state of normal existence.[12] Soma
was conceived of as ruling over the waters and was often coupled with
Agni. Soma has been connected with the sun in the *Rg Veda* but is
connected with the moon in the *Brahmanas*: plants and herbs, indeed
– which Soma must surely be – are mainly connected with the moon
rather than the sun.[13]

Indra

Indra was the Lord of the Thunderbolt and the most popular deity in
the *Rg Veda*. Unlike some of the other deities he is much anthropomorphized. It is he who is portrayed as overcoming the strongholds of
the indigenous people of India, the *dasyus* or *dasas*, when the Aryans first
arrived on the scene. In one important myth he slays the dragon Vrtra
in order to release the pent up waters of existence, perhaps symbolic
of allowing the whole of manifest existence to flow forth from the
state of chaos. He was the supreme *soma* drinker and the ideal Aryan
warrior:

> He was a paradigm of the human qualities the Aryan most admired:
> vigor, enthusiasm, strength, courage, success in battle, gluttony, and
> drunkenness.[14]

This illustrates clearly the rather human nature of this popular deity. He
was closest to the Aryan man, the most anthropomorphic and easily
propitiated deity:

> For the hymns of praise and the songs of praise make you grow great,
> Indra,
> And you bring happiness to the singer of praises.[15]

As the dispenser of rain Indra bestowed fertility on the land, but in
many ways he was aligned with Agni for he represented the fire aspect
in space – lightning and thunder. He was also alligned with cosmic
fire and therefore with the deity Surya.[16] As the king of the gods he

was youthful, active, virile, energetic, and was renowned for his sexual prowess. He was the ideal warlord and warrior – the *Ksatriya* at his best in Aryan eyes. Perhaps Indra was too this-worldly for, despite becoming less active and more dignified as the Vedic period progressed, he was destined to become a very minor deity in the post-Vedic period.

Varuna

Varuna, one of the Adityas, was somewhat different to the other deities. He was the universal monarch and the safe-guarder of cosmic law, *rta*. While he was not a creator god, he kept creation in order and was much more removed from humankind than the other deities for no one – either on earth or in heaven – could offend the laws of the cosmos without incurring the punishment of Varuna. He was absolute sovereign over creation: he made the sun shine in the heavens and the winds were his breath. The rivers, flowing at his command, were hollowed out by him; he made the depths of the sea, caused the sun to rise and set, the stars to shine, and the earth to have life. Since he was omniscient and omnipresent there was no corner of the world where someone could hide from him and he was therefore feared because he could punish sin. He was quite different from a deity like Indra for his character was more moral; indeed, he was the embodiment of moral order and had to be approached with utmost purity and sinlessness. Unlike so many of the other deities he could not be propitiated through sacrifice: only moral purity could win the favour of Varuna. He was feared as much for any unwitting sins that were committed as conscious and deliberate ones:

> O Varuna, whatever the offence may be which we as men commit against the heavenly host,
> When through our want of thought we violate thy laws, punish us not,
> O God, for that iniquity.[17]

But despite his punishment of the iniquities of humankind Varuna could be pleaded to for forgiveness:

> If we have cheated like gamblers in a game, whether we know it or really do not know it, O God, cast all these offences away like loosened bonds.
> Let us be dear to you, Varuna.[18]

There is a profound theism reflected in this verse, but also the idea that it may be possible to overcome sin by appeal to Varuna even after trespasses had been committed. This suggests that the law of the cosmos, *rta*, may not have been so rigidly conceived of at this early stage and that Varuna himself who oversaw its function, had the power to bend its laws in some cases if he saw fit.

Rudra

Rudra, 'The Red One' or 'Howler', was a relatively unimportant god in Vedic times but was destined to become one of the great Gods of Hinduism. In the *Vedas* he is depicted as a ruddy, swarthy man with a wild temper and the murderous temperament of a wild beast. He rode a boar and was a robber god, the lord of thieves. He was also the divine archer who shot arrows of death and disease at gods, men and cattle. He thus personified the dangerous elements of nature; indeed, he was equated with the terrible, destructive form of Agni. In the *Atharva Veda* he is called Pasupati ,'Lord of Cattle', and his association with animals here is reminiscent of the so-called Proto-Siva of the Harappan culture. His unusual nature has caused some to suggest that he was a pre-Aryan deity, perhaps a Dravidian god.[19] But if Rudra's roots lie in the past in ancient India, there is much in his character which points forward to the character of Siva, in particular, the paradox of opposites in his nature. For not only was Rudra the cause of death and disease, he was also the divine physician who took away ailments inflicted by other gods. Thus his gracious hand is said to give wealth and bring comfort.[20] In many ways he symbolizes the dualities of life – its good and bad, happiness and sadness and so on, just as all opposites are united in the deity Siva.

Prajapati

Prajapati was the 'Lord of Beings'. He was Purusa – the huge primeval man who sacrificed himself to form the universe. He was thus the creator of all things; even the gods were his children, and in later Hinduism he becomes the creator god Brahma. The concept of a being such as Prajapati, although representing only one of the many creation myths in Hinduism, is important because of its suggestive panentheism, the belief that all things come forth from one ultimate source and are of the same essence as that source and yet, the source is greater than its created parts. Thus, the *Rg Veda* states:

> This Purusa ia all that hath been and all that is to be:
> The Lord of Immortality which waxes greater by food.

So mighty is his greatnesss; yea, greater than this is Purusa
All creatures are one-fourth of him, three-fourths eternal life in heaven.[21]

Surya and Savitr: the solar deities

Surya and Savitr are two prominent solar deities. Surya is the sun who drives across the sky in his flaming chariot. Savitr is the sun in its nature as stimulator and life-giver in existence. The most sacred verse in the *Vedas*, the *Gayatri mantra*, is dedicated to this god:

May we attain that excellent glory of Savitr the God:
So may he stimulate our prayers.[22]

So sacred are these words that they can only be spoken by the twice-born classes (*dvija*). They are the words which devout Hindus say each morning as they rise and they are used in all religious ceremony. Another solar deity who should be mentioned in this context is Visnu. He was only a minor deity in the Vedic period, indeed he is mentioned in only six hymns. He was noted because he was able to cover the earth, air and heaven in three strides. But like Rudra he was destined to become one of the greatest deities of Hinduism.

Yajna

The whole fulcrum of Vedic religion was the sacrificial ritual known as *yajna*. There were two kinds of sacrificial ritual: the official *srauta* sacrifice which was attended by many priests and the domestic sacrifice of the home which was attended by only one priest, the *purohit*. Fire was central to sacrificial ritual and animal sacrifice was immensely important. At some of the major *yajna* ceremonies such as the *asvamedha* sacrifice, hundreds of animals were sacrificed; indeed, the greater the number the more powerful and efficacious the ritual. Human sacrifice also played a part in the rituals. The whole point of *yajna* was to propitiate the gods in order that they would gratify the needs of the worshippers. As long as the gods were happy, they would reward the worshippers with what they needed most in life – cows in milk, progeny, victory in war and longevity. For the first time the cow became important in this period, not sacred in any way, as in later Hinduism,[23] but the symbol of wealth. For the Vedic man cows were 'the "real life" substratum of the goods of life'.[24] It is therefore evident that on one level the gods were seen as the providers of material good fortune, something reflected in the goal of *artha* in the second *asrama*, the life of the householder, in later Hinduism. Organ rather aptly says that:

> The Vedic *devas* are givers; they are used as the source of the goods of life rather than adored for their intrinsic worth.[25]

Yet there is evidence of some deeper meanings behind this purely mercenary approach to the deities. The very fact of heightened religious experience through partaking of *soma* should suggest that there were higher levels to *yajna*. Daniélou makes the point that *yajna* served the function of 'bringing man into contact with the higher states of being, the deities',[26] and this is an important point, for people, priests and gods attended the *yajnas together*, it was a participatory ritual. It was also participatory in another sense, particularly as the Vedic period proceeded. The sacrifice of Purusa, recorded in the tenth *mandala* of the *Rg Veda*, and which had given rise to the four classes and all creation, came to be recreated by the priests in the sense of a ritualistic re-participation in the original creative process. The creative energies necessary for existence and the prevalence of Aryan society were renewed and continued by the *yajnas*: through the ritual the powers that maintained life in that original sacrifice were recharged. The priests, then, participated in an *ongoing* creation through *yajna*. Important, too, is the fact that by personifying the fundamental powers of human and cosmic existence, the deities enabled the Aryans to make sense of those forces and elements in life, giving meaning to them in daily life – and this shifts the emphasis slightly from the purely propitiatory aspect of the religion.

It was the emphasis on priestly involvement in *yajna* which initiated the real rise of *Brahmanism*. In the process of time the *yajnas* became more and more elaborate and, given the crucial role of replenishing creation on the one hand and the propitiation of the gods for the wealth and stability of Aryan life on the other, the rituals had to be performed to perfection. Many priests were involved: the *hotr* 'reciter' priests were those who recited the hymns of the *Rg Veda*; the *udgatr* 'chanter' priests were those who specialized in the chants from the *Sama Veda*; the *adhvaryu* 'officiater' priests were those who took care of the ritualistic aspects in association with the *Yajur Veda*. It was the *Brahmin* priests who came to be associated with the *Atharva Veda* but they were also responsible for overseeing the whole ritual and therefore had knowledge of all its aspects. They had to make certain that everything was correctly done, otherwise the replenishing of creation and the propitiation of the gods could go hopelessly wrong and the results for Aryan life would have been disastrous. It was believed that the sun itself could not rise without the appropriate, correct religious ritual. It was these *Brahmin* priests who emerged as the most powerful priestly element becoming indispensable to correct ritual performance. Indeed, *brahmans* were originally 'magically potent formulas'[27] but the *Brahmin* priests *themselves* became the medium for magical manipulation – hence their association with the incantational aspects of the *Atharva Veda*. The priestly practices set down in the *Brahmanas*, the priestly commentaries on *Rg Vedic* ceremony, reflect the complexity of ritual and the rigid conformity to precise action (*karman*). Some forms of *yajna* became so elaborate that the ceremony took as long as a year. The *Brahmins* were conceived of as the only agents who were able to manipulate the gods, and if they could have this effect on divine forces they could also manipulate their enemies in the same way. Their power, thus, became largely unchecked and they were feared as much for their effective power over Vedic society – from king down to the most servile – as for their religious powers.

Rta

At the very core of the universe was *rta* – the regulating force of the cosmos. Varuna, as we have seen, was its guardian and punished those who were not in line with it. *Rta* represented order, not only in the rhythm of the planets, the cycle of the seasons and the world of nature, but in all aspects of the life of the universe including the social and moral life of humankind. It is the right path for things, the cosmic norm or pulse which regulates existence, set in place by Varuna:

> King Varuna hath made a spacious pathway for the Sun wherein to travel.[28]

Nothing can overstep the correct path without incurring on the micro-cosmic level the punishment of Varuna, and on the macrocosmic level, disturbance of cosmic norms. So even the gods had to conform to *rta*. It is a very important concept, for it was the precursor of the major Hindu concept of *dharma*, 'what is right', but it is also important in that it was an impersonal force which was more fundamental than any of the deities. Basham depicted it as 'a concept which was perhaps the highest flight of Rg Vedic thought'[29] and it certainly points the way forward to more speculative thought. *Rta* is a principle and certainly not an anthropomorphic deity, as some have suggested.[30] *Rta* does not act, it rather *is* and it is by upholding *rta*, by following the course of *rta*, that the rewards of life are gained and a secure and happy afterlife achieved. Griffith's translation of *rta* as *eternal Law* suggests this well;[31] it is the Law which gives order to all existence:

> it is both the ordered universe as it is in itself and the order that pervades it; and this order is as applicable to the moral conduct of men as it is to the macrocosm of heaven and earth.[32]

Importantly, too, *rta* has a certain unifying aspect in a very abstract way, and this kind of metaphysical speculation on the more abstract principle which may lie beyond the deities was a particular feature of the later Vedic period.

Monotheistic trends

The later hymns of the *Rg Veda* suggest that the search for the source behind the gods themselves was gaining ground and the seeds of a more speculative kind of religious thought had begun to develop. There was always a tendency in the *Vedas* to blur the distinctive roles of the deities, and there were times when one deity was given the identity of another; Rudra, for example, was the more terrible forms of Agni. But some of the later hymns refer to an indescribable Source such as *Tat Ekam*, 'That One', or simply 'That'. In many ways *rta* is the precursor of such an ultimate reality, but it was not seen as an Absolute. One late *Rg Vedic* hymn, epitomizes this speculative and metaphysical search for this Source. Basham described it as 'one of the oldest surviving records of philosophical doubt in the history of the world,[33] and his translation of the hymn is worth citing in full for its sensitive translation and because the hymn is a superb example of the heights of Vedic thought:

> Then even nothingness was not, nor existence.
> There was no air then, nor the heavens beyond it.
> What covered it? Where was it? In whose keeping?
> Was there then cosmic water, in depths unfathomed?
>
> Then there were neither death nor immortality,
> nor was there then the torch of night and day.

The One breathed windlessly and self-sustaining.
There was that One then, and there was no other.

At first there was only darkness wrapped in darkness.
All this was only unillumined water.
That One which came to be, enclosed in nothing,
arose at last, born of the power of heat.

In the beginning desire descended on it –
that was the primal seed, born of the mind.
The sages who have searched their hearts with wisdom
know that which is is kin to that which is not.

And they have stretched their cord across the void,
and know what was above, and what below.
Seminal powers made fertile mighty forces.
Below was strength, and over it was impulse.

But, after all, who knows, and who can say
whence it all came, and how creation happened?
The gods themselves are later than creation,
so who knows truly whence it has arisen?

Whence all creation had its origin,
he, whether he fashioned it or whether he did not,
he, who surveys it all from highest heaven,
he knows – or maybe even he does not know.[34]

Wendy O' Flaherty justifiably says of this hymn:

> in many ways, it is meant to puzzle and challenge, to raise unanswerable
> questions, to pile up paradoxes[35]

and this in fact was what the Vedantic period, the end of the Veda, did
so well.

Vedic deities gradually came to be recognized as different dimensions
of One underlying relaity – the ground of all being – and this realization
led the Vedic poets to come to accept the fusion of all the deities into
one (*visvedevah*) and to look beyond them to the source of all existence
in a very monotheistic way:

> Kindled in many a spot, still One is Agni;
> Surya is One though high o'er all he shines.
> Illuminating this All, still One is Usas.

That which is One has into All developed.[36]

It would need only the identification of each human being with this ultimate One to become a monistic belief system – something which reaches its peak in Vedantic thought and the last line of this hymn in some ways suggests this identification. Certainly at the end of the *Vedas* polytheism gave way to monotheism with the gods and goddesses being conceived of as manifestations of one ultimate Absolute. This is well expressed in the following *Rg Vedic* hymn which states of the One:

> They call him Indra, Mitra, Varuna,
> Agni and he is heavenly noble-winged Garutmat.
> To what is One, sages give many a title: they call it Agni, Yama,
> Matarisvan.[37]

The move to see all things emanating from one source – Time, Heat, Water or Desire for example – certainly lays the seeds for the move to monism in Vedantic philosophical thought and while the Absolute as Brahman does not emerge in the *Vedas*[38] the trend towards its conception is clear.

Alongside the Indus valley culture the Aryan religion supplied the other major foundation for later Hinduism. While the complex ritualism of Vedism no longer obtains aspects of it were important enough to have survived to the present day and can be found in the ceremonies of life-cycle rites and many aspects of temple worship. Hindus regard Vedism as the authentic roots of their religion which still contain the eternal wisdom of existence, the timeless truths of the universe. Over the centuries the Aryan religion spread throughout India to Sri Lanka in the far south. The different shades of Hinduism evolved from the interchange of beliefs and practices between the indigenous population and the Aryan people, and with Hinduism's remarkable ability to accommodate different ideas alongside each other rather than assimilate and syncretize them, the many forms of Hinduism evolved.

14

The Vedanta

From the unreal lead me to the real, from darkness lead me to light, from death lead me to immortality.

Brhadaranyaka Upanisad [1]

Meaning of the term Vedanta

The end of the Vedic period is given the special term *Vedanta*. This term means 'end of the *Vedas*', the word *anta* meaning 'end'. The word *anta* can also mean end in the sense of fulfilment and this is a very apt idea in relation to the Vedanta for the scriptures which the period produced were believed to have been the fulfilment of all knowledge, especially since it was believed that they brought out the real meaning behind the earlier Vedic ritual and scriptural material. Vedantic thought is thus rather different from earlier Vedic thought. Lott has described the Vedanta as 'the most important of India's living conceptual systems' [2] and, while his remark is intended more for the systems of philosophy which rose out of the Vedanta, it serves also as an appropriate statement regarding the fundamental importance of the Vedanta for all Hinduism. It is because the Vedanta deals with the nature of the Absolute, Brahman, that it has provided the foundation for so much subsequent belief in Hinduism as a whole.

The *Upanisads*

Just as the Vedic period is characterized by the scriptures of the period – the *Vedas* – so the Vedanta is characterized by the *Upanisads*, collections of writings from original oral transmissions which have been aptly described as 'the supreme work of the Indian mind', [3] and 'the cornerstone of Indian philosophy'.[4] The usual translation of this word is 'sitting close to', presumably a *guru*, in order to hear the wisdom of one who had cognized the fundamental truths of the universe. Such *gurus* were forest dwellers who departed to the seclusion of an *asram* in the forest in order to contemplate the great metaphysical questions about life. They followed the trend set by the *rsis* or 'seers' in the Vedic period and were thus part of a continuous, evolving tradition. Their pupils or *chelas* sat around them in the shade of a tree, listening to their teachings and engaging in dialogue with them. The *Upanisadic* literature contains a considerable amount of such dialogue between disciple and *guru* and the translation 'sitting close to' is therefore a very apt one. However, the word *upanisad* is a compound one and the roots which compose it can have a variety of meanings. Dandekar, for example, suggests a meaning 'placing side by side' or 'equivalence, correlation', and this would reflect the *Upanisadic* theme of equating all things in life as of one basic essence.[5] Attractive, too, is the interpretation put forward by Alain Daniélou. He suggests that the word can be translated as 'near approach' suggesting a 'near approach' to the Absolute, Brahman. This, indeed, would reflect the main trend of *Upanisadic* thought.[6] Then, again, the *Upanisads* are essentially *esoteric* teachings, secretive teachings which are only for the initiated, and some disciples had to wait patiently for many years before they were deemed worthy by their teachers to receive them. Deussen, therefore, saw the word *upanisad* as expressing the idea of 'secret'.

The *Upanisads* were written from about 800–400 BCE, though scholars vary in their dating of the material. They were thus composed over a long period of time and do not represent a coherent body of information or one particular system of belief. There are contradictions and inconsistencies in their teachings but there is much commonality of thought too. Rohit Mehta is one author who suggests that there is a wholeness to the material of the *Upanisads*. They deal, he says, with *summits* of thought, leaving the details to be pieced in by pupils on their own journeys to the real, to the light and to immortality.[7] The authors of the *Upanisads* were not, as would be expected, solely from the priestly class; indeed it was mainly *Ksatriyas* who set up *asrams* in the forest.[8] The asrams were often associated with a different *Veda – Rg, Sama, Yajur* or *Atharva* – and were thus connected with different schools of Vedic thought. The authors of the *Upanisads* were not interested in the kind of religious ritualism which obtained in Vedic society – indeed, they could hardly be expected to maintain this in the forest setting. They were poets prone to what has been described as 'sheer flashes of spiritual radiance'[9] and their aim was to guide their disciples to the point of liberation which they themselves had reached:

> the poet knows well that if poetry takes us away from a lower reality of daily life it is only to lead us to the vision of a higher Reality even in this daily life, where limitations give way for the poet to the joy of liberation.[10]

Thus we should not expect in the *Upanisads* the kind of language and thought of everyday life; the material is designed to push human thought to its very limits, its summits, and beyond.

There are about 250 *Upanisads* but a much smaller number form the main material and thirteen are singled out as presenting the core teaching; but even these have their inconsistencies of thought. It is in the *Upanisads* that we find all the teachings recognized as fundamental to Hinduism – the concepts of *karma*, *samsara* and *moksa*, the concept of Brahman as Absolute, and the synthesis of Brahman with the *atman* – the essence of each entity and being in the phenomenal world. The *Bhagavad Gita* is also considered to be an *Upanisad* because it, too, deals with the nature of the Absolute, Brahman, as well as fundamental aspects such as *dharma* and the paths to Brahman. The *Gita*, however, is normally consigned to the period of classical, devotional Hinduism for discussion.

The path of intuitive knowledge

The Vedantic period should not be considered in total isolation from the previous Vedic period: indeed, the *Upanisads* are, strictly speaking, Vedic scriptures – part of the *sruti* tradition. As was seen in the previous chapter the move towards a more speculative and mystical approach to religion was evident in late Vedic literature. This is particularly the case with the Vedic *Brahmanas*, and the *Aranyakas*, the forest writings, and there are many aspects of these two which are very similar to *Upanisadic* scriptures. This should warn us about seeing the Vedanta solely as a reaction to the *Brahmanism* and ritualism of the Vedic age. While an element of this obtained, it would certainly be true to say that there was a definite trend towards a more philosophical perspective before the *Upanisads*.[12] But the *Upanisads* epitomize this more speculative thought and ask questions about the nature of the self and of Ultimate Reality in a very focused way.

Yet the Vedanta must also be seen partially as a reaction against the ritualism of the *Vedas*. Dandekar observes that the *Upanisads* rose out of 'a kind of intellectual and social revolt against the closed mechanical sacerdotalism sponsored by the Brahmanas'.[13] The *Upanisads* reflect a certain reaction against the polytheism, indeed the theism of the *Vedas* and are much more inward, mystical and meditative. There is an emphasis, not on correct ritualistic practices in terms of sacrificial ritual, chants, incantations and the like, but on intuitive knowledge and introspection: knowledge became the central issue, not ritual. Such knowledge is called *vidya*, or *jnana*, and the way of knowledge – *jnana marga* – became all important in the Vedantic message and is still an established path to *moksa* in Hinduism today. The path of *jnana* is essentially an individualistic one: Mehta puts this well when he depicts this path as an:

> adventurous journey into the land of the Unknown where alone Wisdom can be discovered. This journey has to be unaided, for no teacher can lead a pupil into the realms of the Unknown. The journey to the Unknown is a flight of the alone to the Alone.[14]

The role of the *guru* is to equip the pupil to stand on his own two feet and journey independently, 'transcending the mind with the help of the mind'.[15]

So the knowledge of which the *Upanisads* speak is not knowledge *about* the world and *about* Ultimate Reality. It is knowledge of a deeper kind – intuitive knowledge which can only be experienced at the deepest levels of the self and which, therefore, cannot be taught or learned. The *gurus* of the forest *asrams*, therefore, could only point their pupils in the right direction: without the inner, direct, intuitive experience, knowledge of Ultimate Reality was impossible. It is not difficult to see, then, why the teachings related to such knowledge were esoteric. A pupil had to be at the right point of his personal evolution to be able to experience such truths in the depths of his being. There is no subject or object in the experience of such knowledge, for the egoistic 'I' which we associate with receiving knowledge is not evident. Knowledge of this kind exists in a 'characterless being', not a personality[16] and is a realization of truth in the sense of a 'seeing of it with the soul and a total living in it with the power of the inner being'.[17] In many ways there is a certain simplicity about such knowledge, and yet it is very profound. We spend our lives busying ourselves with all sorts of things and have little time to reflect, to just be, to be still, and to accept the *suchness* and *thusness* of life. This suchness is exemplified well in a beautiful story from the

Chandogya Upanisad in which Satyakama, a boy from a low-caste family, is accepted into the *asram* of a *guru* and given the test, not of meditating on the nature of life and reality, but of taking care of four hundred, badly conditioned cows! But in the simple life which he led as a cowherd in the forest, Satyakama remained focused on Brahman. Mehta describes admirably the simplicity of life which led to depth of knowledge for Satyakama:

> This urge to know Brahman made everything alive so that the whole of nature became his teacher. Then the trees and the flowers, the sun, moon and the stars, the rivers and the streams, the light of day and the darkness of night – all these spoke to him of the nature of Brahman. He felt that all was Brahman. He heard of Brahman in the songs of the birds, he felt the presence of Brahman in all things that surrounded him. He realized that the eye that sees and the ear that hears does so because of Brahman. He felt that the pulsating life around him as also the mind that raises innumerable questions all these are but aspects of Brahman. Satyakama tended the cows and the bulls – but in the midst of this seemingly mundane work, he communed with nature – and in this communion realized that which filled him with joy indescribable.[18]

The story admirably suggests that Brahman is not divorced from life but is in the essence of every moment and can be experienced as such. Not all human beings can be cowherds! But there are moments in life when the individual transcends ordinary existence and experiences – just for a few moments – the kind of oneness of existence known by Satyakama.

Monism

The characteristic philosophy of the Vedanta is monism. This is a sense of *one-ism*, the idea that everything in the cosmos is one. Differentiation between this and that, and the recognition of dualities in the universe, occur only because of ignorance (*avidya*). The *Upanisads* teach that everything comes forth from the same *Ground of all Being* which is Brahman, so everything is, in essence, really the same. The *Svetasvatara Upanisad* tells us that each individual is woman, man, youth, maiden and old man. He or she is the blue-bird, the green parrot, the cloud pregnant with lightning, the seasons and the seas – all things.[19] Such identification with all things is indicative of monism, but as a philosophical principle monism takes this oneness a stage further and states that everything in the cosmos is also *identical* to the *Ground of all Being*, thus the Absolute,

Brahman, and all animate and inanimate matter is one. This is a non-dual theory, sometimes called *advaita*[20] in Hinduism, and it is the rationale behind the main teaching of the *Upanisads*, the total identification of Brahman and the essence of Brahman in all things – *atman*.

Brahman

From what has been said about the Vedic period it can be seen that there is a trend towards the acceptance of an indescribable Absolute. In many ways the concept of *rta*, the cosmic norm, was a precursor of this. *Rta* was conceived of as the rhythmic energy of the cosmos, an indescribable force beyond even the gods themselves. Additionally, the Vedic *rsis* not only came to accept the fusion of all deities into one, but looked beyond them to the *Source* of all existence in a very non-theistic sense. Although the *Upanisads* are inconsistent in their teachings there is a common focus on Brahman as the *Ground of all Being*. Mostly this Brahman is depicted as an impersonal neuter, not something which can be given masculinity or femininity or, indeed, any attributes at all. It is *neti-neti*, 'not this, not this' which is to say that the moment you wish to say it is this or that you have not understood it at all. Two other terms are sometimes used to refer to Brahman – *Atman and Purusa*; the three terms can be used interchangeably. Brahman cannot be known empirically so intuitive knowledge alone brings one to the understanding *that* Brahman exists, but *what* Brahman is defies understanding for Brahman is beyond the conceptions of the human mind. The term *Brahman* comes from the Sanskrit root *brh* meaning 'to burst forth', and this suggests well the concept of Brahman as the *Ground of all Being* from which everything emanates. The root may also suggest the idea 'to grow, increase', reflecting the unlimited nature of Brahman[21] or 'to be strong'.[22] The ideas of bursting forth and of growth and increase suggest the concept of an Unmanifest Source which becomes manifest in order for existence to come into being and therefore the idea that what is manifest is ultimately the same as its unmanifest source – monism.

It is important to realize that Brahman is not a negative *nothingness* but a *no-thingness* and therefore cannot be subject to the kinds of statements which can be made about *things* in the cosmos. The *Brhadaranyaka Upanisad* says that Brahman is not this and not that, is incomprehensible, inde-structible, unattached, unfettered, cannot suffer, cannot be injured[23] – in short, is beyond the causes and effects of phenomenal existence. These terms from the *Brhadaranyaka*, as well as *neti neti*, are all negative terms and this is really the only way in which we can speak of Brahman without confining it to the levels of human thought. But each negative statement is charged with positive suggestion so that Brahman is really conceived of very positively as free from attachment, free from destruction, and so on. Yet in relation to this Reality of Brahman everything else is negative unreality simply because it is destructible, attached, fettered and so on. The *Chandogya Upanisad* depicts this as the *asat* 'non-being' of the world in comparison to the *sat* 'Being' which is Brahman.[24]

Brahman–*atman*

Whenever a totally transcendent and impersonal Absolute such as Brahman is accepted the question has to be raised that if the Absolute is beyond anything that humankind can comprehend then how can it be known in any way? The answer to this question can only be a negative one *unless* there is some part of manifest existence which is linked in some way – even though indescribably so – with the totally transcendent Absolute. It is this link which is so important in the mystical aspects of religion like Vedanta. The *Upanisads* answer the question by identifying the innermost essence of each manifest entity, the *atman*, with the Unmanifest Source, Brahman. It is this principle which is the key to *Upanisadic* thought and which forms the core of Hindu belief. There are times when this relationship between Brahman and *atman* will be dual – the *atman* only being a part of Brahman and not wholly identifiable with It. There are certainly such dualistic tendencies in the *Upanisads* themselves but the main message of the *Upanisads* is a monistic one – Brahman and *atman* is one and the goal of existence was (and still is) the experience of such oneness, the self becoming the Self. The most well-known words which express this principle come from the *Chandogya Upanisad* and they are *Tat tvam asi* 'That art thou'.

The story behind these words is that of Svetaketu, a young boy who at the age of twelve embarked on his period of study with a *guru*, the first *asrama*. When he returned twelve years later at the age of twenty-four, somewhat conceited and arrogant with the amount of knowledge he had acquired, his father, Uddalaka, asked him whether he had requested from his *guru* that instruction 'by which the unhearable becomes heard, the unperceivable becomes perceived, the unknowable becomes known?'[25] Svetaketu's inability to see how such a question could be answered prompts his father to explain that just as there is one substance, clay, from which all clay vessels come, or gold, from which all gold objects

come, so there is one Source, that of Being, from which the world of
not-being is derived. But the examples of clay are easy to be seen and
therefore Svetaketu's father directs his son to more subtle ideas. He asks
his son to say what he can see when he cuts the fruit from a banyan tree
in half. When it reveals the tiny seeds, his father asks him to cut one of
the seeds in two and again say what he can see. This time Svetaketu has
to admit that he can see nothing yet he knows that something within
the seed must cause it to grow to the mighty banyan tree. Uddalaka tells
his son:

> My dear, that subtle essence which you do not perceive, verily, my
> dear, from that very essence this great *nyagrodha* tree exists. Believe
> me, my dear.
> That which is the subtle essence, this whole world has for its self. That
> is true. That is the self. That art thou Svetaketu.[26]

Uddalaka illustrates the same principle by asking his son to place some
salt in water. The following morning he asks his son to bring him the salt
from the water, but of course it has dissolved. And Uddalaka explains to
his son that Pure Being cannot, likewise, be perceived although it is the
essence of the cosmos, the Source of everything in it, and is identical
to the deepest part of the self.

The words *Tat tvam asi* equate *That* as Brahman with the true inner
self, the 'sphere of space in the chasm of the heart',[27] which is the *atman*.
The *Upanisads*, as later Hinduism, differentiate between the embodied self
(*jivatman*) which is perishable, impermanent, and transient, and the real
Self (*atman*) which is permanent. The *atman*, being present in the body
seems to be connected with it, with its desires, aversions, emotions, joys,
sadness and so on. Bahadur[28] gives a very good analogy here of clear glass
(the *atman*) placed on a red cloth (the personality and its involvement
with the world). The glass *seems* red until it is separated from the cloth.
Likewise the self must be freed from its egoistic involvement with the
world in order to know itself as the true Self which is Brahman. But
this true Self can only be experienced within: all the knowledge which
Svetaketu had acquired had brought him no closer to it. Succinctly, then,
the *Upanisads* teach that:

> behind all of the spatial swirl and temporal flux of the world as it is
> experienced by the senses is a subtle, pervasive, timeless, and unchanging
> reality that is identical to the undying essence of the human being as
> well.[29]

It is the spacial swirl and temporal flux of the world which prevent the individual from experiencing the *atman*. The *Upanisads* often state that the only time the pure Consciousness of *atman* is really experienced is in dreamless sleep, albeit in a transient way. The identity of the *atman* to Brahman is often depicted by the rather good analogy of space in a jar and space outside it. The space in the jar is temporarily confined, as the *atman* is confined by the bodily self. But the space in the jar is still the same as the space outside it and when the jar breaks, the space is one, just as *atman* and Brahman are really one. Whatever exists must contain some of this space but is at no second of time separated from the greater space.[30]

Maya

The perspectives we as human beings have of life are dictated by the dualities we see in it. Thus we can only know what good is in relation to bad or evil, light in relation to darkness, what we like in relation to what we dislike and so on. Human beings exist in space and time. It is the spatial aspect which entrenches differentiation between all the dual aspects of the phenomenal world – this as opposed to that, subject as opposed to object, knower as opposed to known. And all human beings see themselves at a point on the track of time, reflecting back on the past, or reaching forward into the future. Few people simply just are – just living in a particular moment – for all but a few fleeting seconds, and the times in which one ceases to differentiate between the phenomena of life are probably confined to dreamless sleep! But Brahman is not only beyond the limitations of space and time, but is *neti neti* – neither this on the one hand nor that on the other; Brahman is beyond all the differentiations of life, and so is the *atman* which is identical to it. Realization of the *atman* can only come about when the mind is stilled, when it is withdrawn from the egoistic movement between dualities which help it make sense of life, and when it is in the *isness* or *suchness* of the moment. The mind is like a screen on which we project images, emotions, spatial conceptions, choices between dualities, and subtle modes of consciousness of which we ourselves may not be aware. It is when the screen is left blank for a moment that the *thusness* of the *atman* is experienced and its changeless Reality (*sat*); for how can the shifting, impermanent patterns we place on the screen be real? So experience of such reality is experience, not of the ordinary consciousness of daily life or the outcomes of unconscious and subconscious processes, but experience of Pure Consciousness (*cit*), an experience which brings the bliss (*ananda*) of identity with Brahman. Nothing illusory can bring happiness: only what is real, the fullness of Brahman, can bring eternal bliss.

> There is one thing that *is*, and only one – the light within, the light in which these pleasures and pains, these fleeting scenes and semblances, come and go, pass into and pass out of being. This primordial light, this light of lights, beyond the darkness of the self-feigned world-fiction, this fontal unity of undifferentiated being, is pure being, pure thought, pure bliss.[31]

Because monism is a non-dual system of belief it denies the dualities of the world as unreal, emphasizing only the oneness of all the cosmos. Such dualities and the plurality and diversity of the world we see around us are illusory or *maya*: indeed, if they are transient and subject to decay and death, how can they be real? But it is precisely the diversity of the world which entices us as individuals, and the more we become involved in it the deeper the involvement with *maya* and the further away we are from Reality. *Maya* thus serves to conceal Brahman like a cloud conceals the sun. An analogy of the famous ninth-century philosopher Sankara illustrates this well. He likened *maya* to a coiled rope on a path which, at late dusk, gives every appearance of a snake. And anyone seeing it would have the very real fears and reactions which such a sight would create. But travelling the same path in the light of day and realizing that the snake was, after all, a rope, removes the illusion and presents what is real: likewise, losing the image of the phenomenal world as real and realizing the reality of Brahman, puts Ultimate Reality into its correct perspective. To suggest that this impermanent, constantly changing world is the only reality is to be living under the delusion of *maya*:

> The sum of migrating forms of life, and of the spheres through which they migrate, is the ever-moving world. Everything in it is coming into being, and passing out of being, but never is.[32]

In the ever-shifting scenes of life, how can there be the permanence which must constitute what is real? Because the *Upanisadic* answer to this question is to deny reality to the phenomenal world, only Brahman is real: all else is *maya*. Importantly, however, *maya* refers to the material world and not to the *essence* of phenomena in the world. It is the essence and not the material which is equated with Brahman. So for each human being it is the *atman* alone which is real; 'Self alone is, and all else only seems to be'.[33]

Theism in the *Upanisads*

What we have in the *Upanisads* is a move away from the polytheism of the *Vedas* to a concept of the non-duality and non-plurality of the world – a concept of oneness, of monism. While most would accept that a monistic belief system is the overriding message of the *Upanisads*, there are some *Upanisads* in which the move towards the conception of deity on a more personal, theistic basis is evident. In particular, the *Svetasvatara Upanisad* extols Rudra-Siva as the transcendent God and the *Katha* features a transcendent Visnu. There is a move here from monism to panentheism, a dual perspective by which the *atman* is still identified with Brahman but only partly so: ultimately God – and here we can use the term God – is greater than all existence, not equated with it. These more theistic *Upanisads* refer to Brahman in its manifest, *saguna*, form as *Isvara* or simply *Isa*, meaning 'Lord'. This transcendent but manifest aspect of the Absolute is describable and is able to be related to on a more personal level. The following verse from the *Svetasvatara Upanisad* illustrates well both the transcendent Brahman as more subtle than the subtle and greater than the great – that is to say beyond human conception – and, the *personal* God of grace:

> Subtler than the subtle, greater than the great is the Self that is set in the cave of the (heart) of the creature. One beholds Him as being actionless and becomes freed from sorrow, when through the grace of the Creator he sees the Lord and His majesty.[34]

However, while there is certainly evidence of theism in the *Upanisads*, especially in the later ones, it is not a move back to the theism of the *Vedas* for there is much more emphasis on the transcendent aspects of the divine than is evident with Vedic deities. The kind of theism which is evident in these later *Upanisads* is more explicit but there are elements of it in other *Upanisads* at times – a typical example of the inconsistencies in Vedantic literature.

The evolution of the self

Given that the ultimate aim in Vedantic thought is knowledge of

Brahman in the deepest, intuitive sense and the fusion of the self with the Self, *atman* with Brahman, it is easy to see why one single lifetime would be insufficient for such realization. The self evolves through an immense period of time, reincarnating from one existence to the next. Experience of *atman* may be glimpsed in one lifetime but life has to be lived *entirely* rooted in *atman*, and the *jiva*, the egoistic self has to be obliterated. Human beings cannot really last one minute without an egoistic thought and every egoistic thought is a *karmic* cause and must have a result – a result which accrues to the I which caused it. All individuals make sense of the world by dfferentiating between this and that, that is to say they are perpetuating the illusory distinctions of *maya* by living life in a world of dualities in which they make egoistic choices and judgements. And it is often the more subtle choices of the mind, even of the subconscious, which cause the individual to perpetuate desire or aversion for one thing as opposed to another. But, as we have seen, Brahman is beyond dualities, at a point where they cease to exist. For an individual to come to that point too, when the dualities of life disappear and all is one, takes millions of reincarnations which Hinduism would view as the logical evolution for each person. Only when the egoistic self, the I, is lost can results of mental or physical actions cease to belong to a person, simply because there is no personality evident to which they can accrue. So 'a person must somehow transcend the results of his own actions'.[35] *Dharma* helps a person to evolve to this point by placing the individual in the life situation most suited to his or her stage of evolution – *varnadharma* 'class *dharma*', *asramadharma* 'stage of life *dharma*' *svadharma* 'one's own *dharma*'. And overriding all are the more cosmic concepts of *sadharanadharma*, the common duties and obligations to one's fellow human beings, and *sanatanadharma*, the eternal law, the universal *dharma*, reminiscent of the older concept of *rta* in the *Vedas*.

Moksa: the final goal

The goal of the Hindu is thus to lose the kind of *karma* which attaches itself to the egoistic self and to have no need to reincarnate. Then, the cycle of *samsara* over, the sages taught that one experiences the unity of all existence and becomes Brahman. This is *sat*, *cit*, and *ananda* (Truth or Being, Pure Consciousness and bliss). Like the ease by which we experience dreamless sleep, *moksa* does not have to be found; it is already there, like a treasure buried in one's own home. The Vedantic sages taught that through the path of knowledge, ascetic withdrawal from the world of the senses, and meditative practices, the evolution of the self could reach the point of realization of Brahman. To know Brahman one has to come to know the emptiness of the fulness of life and the fulness of that emptiness in the bliss of Brahman.

The Vedanta stands in sharp contrast to the previous Vedic period of which, really, it is a part. As a result of the more introspective analyses of the deeper levels of existence, in particular the self, Vedic deities and the ritualism of Vedic religion became less important. Doctrines like *karma* and *dharma* emphasized individual effort for liberation and the Brahman–*atman* synthesis pointed to divinity for every human soul irrespective of the Vedic deities. However, the introspective approach to Brahman did not entirely eschew Vedic ritual,[36] it rather searched for the inner meaning of it, and however philosophical the *Upanisads* were, the importance of scriptural authority (*sruti*) was never denied. The influence which *Upanisadic* thought had on subsequent Hindu beliefs was colossal. The major concepts of *karma, samsara, moksa, atman,* Brahman and the relationship between these last two – indeed so much of what is accepted in Hinduism today – owes its origin to Vedantic thought. Five of the six Hindu orthodox schools of philosophical thought – Vedanta, Samkhya, Nyaya, Vaisesika, Yoga – are based on the Vedanta, while the sixth, Purva Mimamsa, began by being orientated to the more ritualistic earlier Vedic period and later to Vedantic thought. It would be true to say that Vedantic teachings served as the basis of all Hindu thought, the search for the real in the world of the unreal, the search for light in the darkness of the world, and the search for immortality in the face of death.

15

Devotional Hinduism

The move towards theism

Whilst Vedantic thought gave to subsequent Hinduism the substratum of most of its philosophical thought as well as many basic beliefs, the level of its metaphysics must have barely touched the ordinary village people for whom a totally transcendent Absolute such as Brahman must have seemed far less appropriate than the important village deities. We have little evidence to suggest continuity of tradition in village life, simply because it was the official Aryan ideas and rituals which were eventually committed to written form. And while it is almost certain that indigenous religious beliefs and practices must have been accommodated by the Aryans themselves, the evidence for exactly which aspects is uncertain. But it is likely that such aspects as worship of divinity in female form continued at the village level and that the more theistic beliefs in personal deities obtained widely in village life.

The evidence from the *Svetasvatara*, *Katha* and *Isa Upanisads* suggests that theism, albeit of a different kind to that which obtained in the earlier Vedic period, began to emphasize the *saguna* aspects of Brahman, the *manifest* aspects of deity. It is this manifest dimension to divinity which flowered into the whole expression of devotional Hinduism and a theism which allowed for an intensely *personal* relationship between the individual and the divine. The trend towards monism which was witnessed in the *Upanisadic* scriptures of the Vedanta gave way to an overt dualism between God and humankind, and it was this dualism which allowed for expressions of theism ranging from simple anthropomorphism to highly transcendent perspectives of the divine. No longer was the Absolute indescribable. In its manifest form there was no end to attributes it could be given and no end to the number of divine manifestations which emanated from it. It is devotional Hinduism, therefore, which is characterized by the multiplicity of deities which we associate with Hinduism today.

Bhakti

Strictly speaking *bhakti* was a movement or movements in Hinduism characterized by ecstatic devotion to the manifest aspects of Brahman in the form of Visnu or Siva, but the term has come to be used much more generally almost as a synonym for devotional practices in Hinduism: indeed Biardeau has commented that 'For my part, I know of no so-called "local" cult which does not contain the general beliefs of bhakti'.[1] The word *bhakti* comes from the Sanskrit root *bhaj* which means 'to be attached to', 'to resort to' 'to partake of', or 'to share in', 'belong to'.[2] Such concepts express well the idea of the devotee belonging to a particular deity, sharing reciprocal love with that deity and partaking of the grace of the deity. But *bhakti* as a term denotes much more than devotion, for it involves a passionate yearning and ecstatic emotion which is essentially *loving*-devotion, for it implies total surrender of the devotee in loving-devotion to his or her personal deity. It began in the southern parts of India, the less Aryanized Tamil region. Some see its origins as dating back to about the second century CE,[3] but it is certainly articulated in the *Gita* dated to the early centuries BCE, while others consider its real origins to be in the sixth century at the time of the devotional saint poets who epitomize *bhakti*.[4] The origins of *bhakti* as well as its nature as a present phenomenon are well expressed by Lannoy when he says:

> In origin it is a non-Brahman movement of popular religiosity which emerged in South India among classes which were resistant to the pressures of caste hierarchization; it is still very much a living force.[5]

Despite its origin in the south of India it was not exactly a single movement since it manifested itself variously in different sects. The diverse nature of *bhakti* and, indeed, of the devotional aspects of Hinduism in general, are exemplified well in the scriptures themselves. Thus we find a somewhat lofty and controlled view of *bhakti* in the *Bhagavad Gita* appropriate for the conception of Krisna as the deity–warrior of considerable wisdom. This stands in sharp contrast to the perspective of *bhakti* in the *Bhagavat-Purana* which is more intimate and passionate in character, corresponding to the more fun-loving portrayal of the cowherd Krisna.[6]

In character *bhakti* is a dualistic concept, though not exclusively so. It allows for the kind of personal relationship with the divine which has produced what might be called a 'full-blown theism'.[7] It was in many ways a protest against formal religion and was characterized by highly experiential communion with the deity which was not at all emotionally subdued. As such, it was open to all classes and castes and also to women: God became accessible to all, could be loved by all, and all could be recipients of his grace. It was the inner experience of love of the deity which was such an important aspect of *bhakti* but which had its outward expression in ecstatic behaviour of singing and dancing. The ecstacy of communion with God was balanced by the sheer agony of separation from him and, while the deity was viewed with the deepest possible love, he was also viewed with reverence and awe as well as with obedience and humility which, Lannoy suggests, sometimes went as far as 'morbid, self-abasement'.[8]

It is the *Bhagavad Gita* which is the first scripture to highlight *bhakti*, presenting it as one of the most desirable paths to God and to *moksa*. Then, in the sixth and seventh centuries in the south of India *bhakti* reached its high point with the Tamil poets, and a great surge of devotional poetry to Visnu and Siva ensured that the devotional path to God would remain in the hearts of many Hindus. The poets travelled widely singing their poetry in praise of God in the vernacular, so that it was readily accessible to all who would listen. The Saivite poets were called *nayanars* (lords, leaders), while the Vaisnavite poets were called *alvars* 'divers' into religious truth. But such devotionalism was not confined to the south for it spread to the north of India with the same fervour, attracting people of all classes: indeed, one famous poet, Tukaram (1598–1650), was a *Sudra*.

Some see the origins of *bhakti* in the early Vedic period in the kind of devotion offered to deities such as Agni and Varuna who were appealed to in a very personal way and were approached for their bestowal of grace on their devotees. And there must have been similar devotional practices evident at the village level. However, from what we have seen of the nature of *bhakti* and its emphasis on the concept of love, it is better viewed as a distinct phenomenon in Hinduism which may have had some vague roots in the Vedic or pre-Vedic past, but which flowered independently. Moreover, *bhakti*, as devotional aspects of Hinduism today, is characterized by an emphasis on the reciprocal love of devotee to deity and of deity to devotee. This is a quite distinctive characteristic beautifully expressed in the words of Krisna in the *Bhagavad Gita*:

Hear again my supreme and most secret word of all: I love you dearly, therefore I shall speak to you what is for your good.

Fix your mind on me, be devoted to me, sacrifice to me, bow down to me, then I promise you in truth you will come to me, for you are dear to me.

Having abandoned all *dharmas*, take refuge in me alone. I shall liberate you from all evils; grieve not.[9]

This expression of the essential love of God for his devotee is the kind of love which typifies devotional Hinduism. Love is the important relationship between individual and deity in a way in which it never was in the Vedic period and is a love universally available. It is not surprising that the devotional path in Hinduism became so important.

Surrender of the self

While *bhakti* is an aspect of devotionalism it would be true to say that most devotionalism is informed in some way or other by *bhakti*. What characterizes both is a kind of intense theism by which the individual self is transcended through devotion to the divine. The individual must pour out his or her love in total self-surrender to God. Again, we find the emphasis on loss of the egoistic self as in the way of knowledge, *jnana marga*. The idea of surrender (*prapatti*) to the deity is well described in the verses above from the *Gita* and it is this aspect which allows for so much diversity of practice. The singing of hymns in praise of the deity – called *kirtan* in the north and *bhajans* in the south – will take place at home or at the temple, and dancing, repetition of the deity's name or meditation on the deity for example, are kinds of activities by which the individual becomes so absorbed in the deity that the self is surrendered. Devotion to the deity is also expressed in terms of personal human relationships like that of child to parent, parent to child, servant to master, between friends or between lovers. And just as in these relationships the self is often surrendered for the good of the other, so the devotee can surrender the self to God through envisaging God in this way. Vaisnavism, in particular, emphasizes single-pointed surrender on the part of the devotee: 'The soul's destiny, through God's grace, is to eternally worship and enjoy him'.[10]

The importance of *avatars*

Because devotional Hinduism concentrates on the *saguna* aspects of
Brahman, theism is its essential characteristic. At its height such theism
is evident in the concept of the 'descent' of God to the level of
humankind – *avatars*. It is through this concept of *avatars* that the
most anthropomorphic and approachable aspects of the divine are in
evidence, and, judging by the immense popularity of aspects of Hinduism
which centre round the concept of *avatars*, it could surely be claimed that
humankind finds such a concept a very attractive one because it is one
which relates more effectively to human need. It is Visnu who descends
to earth for the purpose of correcting any deviance from *dharma* which
is over-threatening to humankind. And it is the particular *avatars* as
Krisna and Ram around which devotionalism centres for Vaisnavites,
followers of Visnu. Devotionalism is highly varied and for some it will
take the form of worshipping Krisna as a child, lord or parent, or of
worshipping Ram, whose devotion to *dharma* is so exemplary. Whatever
path is chosen, the pouring out of love to the deity is essential.

It is the emphasis on love which is important in much of the *smrti*
literature of the devotional era of Hinduism – in the *Ramayan* the love
of Sita for her husband Ram, and of Laksman for his brother Ram,
and in the *Puranas* in the love of Radha for Krisna. These relationships
serve as examples to the devotee of how a deity can be loved. In some
versions of the *Ramayan*, for example that of Tulsi Das, Sita is portrayed
as the epitome of what a devotee should be – loyal, submissive, devoted,
ardent, and agonized when separated from her husband.[11] But the kind
of love which exists between Krisna and Radha as lovers is a particular
role model for devotees. Such was Radha's ardent love for Krisna that
she abandoned her own husband. Her relationship with Krisna vacillates
between the ecstacy of erotic physical union and agony and desperation
when she is parted from him. So deep is her love for Krisna that Radha
has to overcome every obstacle to their union together. But it was
not only Radha who loved Krisna so ardently, for all the *gopis* loved
him too.

In Bengali devotionalism especially, this kind of intense and constant
love became something to emulate but, importantly, because it was love
for God, it was lifted from the worldly sexual level to a love which
was holy, a love which, if it were sufficiently intense, could result in
moksa.[12] The normal dimensions of *maya* which cloud reality are lost
when devotion to God is at such a depth of intensity. Krisna thus became

the means by which experience of earthly love could be transformed into love of the divine and could bring experience of divine love: he was the very embodiment of love and joy, a deity who is sheer delight to all people and, importantly, who is devoted to his worshippers even though he may be hidden and separated from them. Thus, passionate longing for God can bring the devotee to realization of *moksa* as much as the more introspective path of *jnana* which we examined in relation to Vedanta. The anthropomorphic appeal of this concept of God is considerable. Krisna is a *beautiful* God, smiling, charming, handsome and winning, a God whom the devotee, the *bhakta*, would want to remember, return to, be with forever, and desire. The self is forgotten in the intensity of love for God and people could come to know the divine through the medium of earthly love transformed to the dimensions of sacred love:

> In the history of Krsnaism profane love, sensual, human longing, became clearly related to sacred love. Within the Krisna-cults a love mysticism, a love-symbolism, developed. The human and the divine became inextricably interwoven in love, in *bhakti*, no longer *bhakti* simply as 'devotion', but *bhakti* as fervent, passionate love. . . . The mythology of Visnu incarnated as the irresistible and playful cowherd-lover was a sacralization of human love. God became understood as transcendent and yet immanent, wholly distinct from the self and dearly personal, to be desired with all one's heart. Passionate, human love, if it was directed toward Krsna, was sacred.[13]

The love affair between Radha and Krisna, therefore, is a symbol of the ideal relationship between the soul and God, in a love which is reciprocal. Union between the soul and God is the natural blissful state of the soul which, in view of its true nature as *atman* is but a manifestation of the divine. This is what Radha experienced in union with Krisna.[14] Because all souls, the *atman*, are considered to be female there is no difficulty in equating the inner soul with Radha. So men, too, are able to interiorize the same kind of ardour and passion which Radha had for Krisna, but as some have pointed out it is not easy to do.[15] However a converse situation by which male devotees can view the Goddess in any of her forms as a lover, is not acceptable.[16] The aim of the devotees is, as Kinsley aptly states, 'to uncover the Radha dimension within themselves'.[17]

Devotional scriptures

The scriptures of devotional Hinduism belong to the *smrti* tradition,

smrti meaning 'memory'. Such scriptures were written by sages who
'remembered' the words which God had spoken to them. *Smrti* literature
consists of:

Vedangas	rules on ritual, astronomy, morals, grammar and phonetics, and also the *Dharma Sastras*, the 'Law Books'.
Darsanas	writings on the six philosophical schools of religious thought.
Itihasas	literally *this indeed it was*; these are historical narratives, and both the *Ramayan* and the *Mahabharat* belong in this context, though they hardly seem like historical accounts.
Upavedas	writings which have been appended to the *Vedas*, for example the *Ayurveda* which is concerned with medicine.
Tantras	esoteric, mystical teachings.
Agamas	writings which are pertinent to specific Hindu sects such as Vaisnavites or Saivites. They may fall into the category of *tantric* writings because they are rather mystical and require a *guru* in order to understand them.
Upangas	literature concerned with ritual and logical thought.
Puranas	eighteen major works which are mainly highly devotional and are generally dedicated to the various main deities of Hinduism.

Devotional belief and practices are involved particularly with the *Itihasas*
and the *Puranas*. Indeed, there is much similarity and even synonymity
between these two types of literature. The latter are important scriptures
for extolling the various deities. Visnu, Siva and Sakti are given supremacy
in different *Puranas*. While they deal with complex concepts such as time,
creation and dissolution, the cosmos and the nature of the world, they are
also guidelines for life, and are immensely loved by the ordinary Hindu as
much as the learned. It is in the *Bhagavat Purana* that the life of Krisna is
related, with wonderful stories about his birth, childhood and manhood.
It is the *Puranas*, too, which contain detailed accounts of the *avatars* of
Visnu, where they stretch well beyond the usual ten.

The narratives contained in the *Puranas* are immensely attractive and
the use of narrative for the medium of teaching religious ideas appeals
to Hindus everywhere, being at once easy to understand, yet at the
same time containing levels of thought which cater for different stages
of consciousness: thus each individual can respond to them in his or her
own way. But the *Puranas* should not be considered as totally divorced
from the Vedic scriptures for they are believed to complement Vedic

teaching by presenting it in narrative form. The *Upanisads* taught the way of *jnana*, intuitive knowledge of the divine and withdrawal from the world, but the *Puranas* extol the life of the householder and demonstrate that the path to God can be one that does not exclude everyday life, a factor which is very valid for the ordinary Hindu. And in devotional Hinduism, most Hindus would favour the particular *Purana* or *Puranas* which feature their chosen deity, where that deity in question is portrayed as supreme over all others. Hindus see nothing unusual in the concept that supremacy is accorded Visnu in one *Purana*, Siva in another and the Mother Goddess in another. The manifest forms of Brahman are many, but ultimately all are Brahman and whatever form in which the worshipper wishes to approach the divine, then Brahman takes that form.

It would be erroneous to consider that devotional Hinduism is centred entirely on the most anthropomorphic conception of deity in the form of *avatars*. Apart from a host of local deities who are the focus of devotional practices, the great ascetic God Siva also features widely in devotional Hinduism and Saivism is, in the main, a devotional phenomenon. The intense personal devotion between a *bhakta* and the deity, and the ardent love of Siva, is very well expressed in a twelfth-century poem by a Saivite woman saint, Mahadevi, who betrothed herself to Siva and wrote of him:

> He bartered my heart,
> looted my flesh,
> claimed as tribute
> my pleasure,
> took over
> all of me.
>
> I'm the woman of love
> for my Lord, white as jasmine.[18]

The theism of the *Bhagavad Gita*

The *Gita* was the earliest scripture in which the devotional approach to God, specified as *bhakti*, is featured. In calling the *Gita* a *upanisad*, Hindus do not consider it to be separate from the *Vedas* but its overt theism and devotional tone which incorporate a very personal approach to the divine make it aptly placed in the context of epics such as the *Mahabharat* and the *Ramayan*. Yet the *Gita* is clearly not a historical narrative for in its content

Krisna as the charioteer of Arjun put forward profound spiritual teaching which has been a source of inspiration and understanding of the divine to Hindus everywhere. In this sense, then, it is appropriately referred to as a *upanisad*. It has been variously dated from anything from the sixth to the first or second centuries BCE, but most favour the latter. Not only was it the first scripture in which *bhakti* was attested, it was the first scripture, as Hardy notes, 'to suggest a sufficient theology of Krisna to make it a religious system "Krsnaism"'.[19]

But it is not only the devotional path to God, *bhakti marga*, which is featured in the *Gita*. The paths of *jnana* 'knowledge', and *karma* 'action', are also prominently portrayed, while, overarching all ways to God is the fundamental yogic discipline of yoking the senses. *Jnana marga* has been dealt with in the context of the Vedanta but *karma marga* needs some mention at this point. In many ways it is one which is ideally suited to the particular predicament of Arjun. The fact that *karma* means 'action' tells us immediately that *karma marga* is not a path to God which is divorced from the world: indeed it involves action in the world in every way, but with one important difference. The action involved with the way of *karma* is egoless action, that is to say, the kind of action which is undertaken without any desire or aversion or without any consideration for the fruits of the action; it is an action not carried out with a sense of I. It is not actions which produce good or bad *karma* for the future but the ego which is attached to the actions, and its accompanying desires and aversions and attachments to their results.

Commentators on the *Gita* usually stress the predominance of one path as opposed to others in the message of the text. It is a complex writing and the fact that Sankara, probably the greatest of Hindu philosophers, could interpret the *entire* text from a monistic viewpoint of total identity of the self with Brahman, thus elevating the path of *jnana*, should warn against the acceptance of either of the other two paths of *bhakti* or *karma* as predominant. Adopting *karma marga* as the main teaching would answer Arjun's dilemma very well in that if he is able to do his duty as a *Ksatriya* and fight in the coming battle with no sense of ego, then no results of his actions can be attached to him. And his questions to Krisna at the beginning of the *Gita* reveal that it is precisely the results of his actions in fighting a fratricidal war which are to the front of his mind. But many commentators suggest that it is the path of *bhakti* – loving devotion to the personal God Krisna – which is the path favoured by the *Gita*, and there is much in the text to support this. While there are certainly passages which could be interpreted monistically, the emphasis on devotion to, and focus on, Krisna is a recurrent theme:

> I am easily obtainable, Partha, by him who thinks of nothing else, constantly remembers me daily, an ever-integrated Yogin.[20]

Yet it could also be claimed that it is the focus on Krisna that is the teaching which unites all paths. It is *surrendering* the self to Krisna which is important irrespective of the path that is followed – loving-devotion, egoless action, or intuitive knowledge of the *atman* within through withdrawal from the world, meditation and ascetic practices. It is the surrendering of the self through focusing on Krisna which brings realization of Brahman, irrespective of the chosen path. Krisna makes himself a manifest object which wills the soul towards him. Biardeau, who calls the *Gita* a 'gospel of bhakti'[21] says that:

> God, in making himself accessible to his worshipper and granting him his grace, becomes the object of desire, the one which suppresses all other desires.[22]

This brings about what Biardeau describes as a 'transfer of man's whole capacity for desire onto God'.[23] It is this kind of thought which is so typical of the devotional approach to God in Hinduism by which the devotee in unqualified love of God comes to know him and to be one with him.

The concept of God in the *Gita* is that of a loving God whose love for humankind is available to all whatever their caste, sex or status in life, or even if they worship other deities with complete devotion. The *Gita* made devotional Hinduism available to the old and young, the intellectual and the slower-minded and in its many levels of thought each can glean from it what his or her level of consciousness allows.

The grace of God

Another important aspect of the concept of God in devotional Hinduism is that of the grace (*prasad*) of God. This should not be seen quite in the Western sense as a wiping clean of the slate of sins of individuals, the overriding of all past *karma*, but more as a grace which provides every opportunity in manifest creation for the devotion of humankind to God. Strictly speaking, the grace of God is not so much something which can be petitioned for, as something which can be *experienced* at moments when the ego is lost, at moments of desirelessness – something to be celebrated and not requested. Yet, at the level of the village deities, particularly the less benign female deities, the grace of the deity is an important issue for the welfare of the village as much as for the individual, and it is perhaps at this level that there is something of a request for the grace of the deity through devotional practice.

Monotheism and panentheism

The nature of God in devotional Hinduism is very different from the monistic conception of a totally transcendent Absolute which we saw put forward by some of the major *Upanisads*. In devotional Hinduism there is an *involvement* with the deity and this is an involvement which includes the human emotion of love. In devotional Hinduism devotees have a personal focus for worship with deities which can be described and which are involved with creation in a personal way, helping humankind on the many paths to God realization. It is devotional Hinduism which pervades popular religion, providing many varied ways in which the divine can be approached. But since the Unmanifest source, Brahman, is manifest in a multiplicity of forms within the cosmos, this allows an individual to pour out his or her devotion to the aspect of deity which is dearer to that individual and which best suits his or her personality and level of consciousness. While it cannot be denied that caste background may have something to do with the choice, most individuals would have an *ista-devata* 'chosen deity' – a personal deity who will be the main focus of devotion.

While the abundance of possible manifestations of Brahman has brought about what seems to be a polytheistic approach to the divine, few Hindus would agree with this term as an appropriate designation of the religion in any of its dimensions. Devotional Hinduism is monotheistic for two reasons. The first is that all deities are, ultimately, Brahman – they are all one – and, secondly, it is practically impossible for an individual to give equal attention to all deities; one will be the chosen object of devotion above all others in a monotheistic approach. Even though five deities are invoked in all Hindu worship – Ganesh, Surya, Siva, Devi, and Narayan (Visnu) – these *pancayatana*, as they are called, are a prelude to worship of the individual's chosen deity. To pour out devotion on a deity with total surrender and total love, one can really only have one deity, one's *ista devata*. But at the same time it is possible to recognize that the *ista devata* of another will be a different mainifestation of the divine. Even when the same deity as another is worshipped, it may well be a different form of that deity:

> the bhakta is almost always more particularly attached to a given form of the deity. He worships Visnu, but the Visnu of Srirangam rather than another, the linga of Siva, but that of Cidambaram or Kalahasti. Or he is a devotee of Venkatesvara at Tirupati, of Virhoba at Panharpur . . . all the themes evoked around *bhakti* give rise to a divine form and a particular feeling on the part of the worshipper.[24]

This kind of focus on a particular aspect of the divine in devotional Hinduism has been appropriately termed 'informal monotheism' by Lorenzen.[25]

In contrast to the monism of the *Upanisads*, devotional Hinduism maintains a theistic stance of a personal relationship with the divine and a dualism between worshipper and deity. *Bhakti* opened up this kind of personal relationship, stressing the *saguna*, manifest, aspects of Brahman rather than Brahman as *nirguna*. The dualism between divine and human which is indicative of such devotional theism is retained at *moksa*: the individual *atman* does not become God but is a part of God. This makes each entity a fraction of the divine and there is much to suggest in devotional Hinduism that God is always greater than the totality of the cosmos.[26] This is panentheism, and when all is drawn back to its unmanifest source, God remains, though all else ceases to exist. However, for the individual who can remain constantly and passsionately devoted to his or her chosen deity, surrendering the self to God in every way and in every moment, release from *samsara* is achieved for the bliss of everlasting communion with God. The words of the poet Rabindranath Tagore depict admirably the communion of the soul with the divine when the self is surrendered:

> I feel that all the stars shine in me.
> The world breaks into my life like a flood.
> The flowers blossom in my body.
> All the youthfulness of land and water smokes like an incense
> in my heart; and the breath of all things plays on my thoughts
> as on a flute.[27]

16

Unity in Diversity

So how does one conclude an introduction to a religion which is as complex as Hinduism? And are there any real conclusions to such a diverse phenomenon? And where does the reader go next and with what kind of forward vision? To answer the first two questions we need to look at two areas: the first, the principle of accommodation of beliefs and practices in Hinduism, and the second, the unity behind the presence of dualities.

Accommodation

It is the accommodation of new and different beliefs and practices alongside established patterns of religion which is perhaps the most important factor informing the multiplicity and diversity of religious expressions which make up what we call Hinduism today. And such accommodation has a long history, stretching back through the centuries to pre-Harappan times. It has been facilitated somewhat by a mainly village culture, and, also, by the sheer size of area over which Hinduism has been and is evident. The usual picture of inter-village and tribal warfare which has characterized the early stages of some religions seems to be mainly absent from the Indian scene. This ability to accommodate new beliefs and practices displays a remarkable tolerance for the viewpoint of others. This is not to say that resistance has always been absent. Certainly the influence of immigrant religion such as the Aryan or Muslim incursions in India met with resistance, and southern India, in particular, resisted Aryanization. Notably the Buddha came from the Sakya kingdom of north-east India where there was marked resentment of the rigid *Brahmanism* of Hinduism and of the class system it promulgated. This was an area where people were sufficiently independent and unorthodox to be less likely to accept established traditions. But in the main, Hindus are tolerant enough to put pictures of the leaders and founders of faiths other than their own in their temples, and to allow the rise of new deities, new temples, new shrines, when a new expression of their religion emerges.

Yet despite the diversity which such accommodation has allowed there is a very profound underlying unity in the concept of the manifestation of all existence from one, ultimate, *Ground of all Being*. The apparent diversity of belief and practice serves to allow an approach to divinity in whatever way suits individual evolution and the recognition of this fact, alongside the notion that the *One*, Brahman, can take a multiplicity of forms, supplies a certain unity to the apparent surface diversity.

Unity of apparent dualities

From the metaphysical levels of the religion to the simplest, Hinduism is characterized by what seem to be opposing viewpoints. The concept of deity itself is one of total non-manifestation which is *nirguna* and yet manifestation in a variety of forms as *saguna*. So on the one hand we have a metaphysical concept of a totally transcendent Absolute and on the other the *avatar* as the epitome of anthropomorphic theism. Yet the Hindu sees no disparity here because all is ultimately one, Brahman. Then again, the cyclical conception of all existence, both in the microcosm of the world and the macrocosm of the cosmos, means that dual concepts of creation and dissolution become unified. For what is created must, ultimately, cease to exist in a world of flux and transience, but equally so, what ceases to exist is reborn again, from the universe to the tiniest flower. Life is death and death is life; all that is born must die and what dies will be reborn. Siva, as we saw in *Part One* exemplifies this as the dissolving force in existence who at the same time is the colour of life and creation – white. And Visnu, the creating, preserving force of life is the dark colour of death: the one prefigures the other in a never-ending cycle.

Sometimes quite opposing ideas have been accommodated side by side. The belief in *karma* and *samsara* is maintained alongside a belief in ancestors and the existence of heaven and hell. No paradox is seen here: the latter concepts of heaven and hell are simply places to which the dead will go, depending on their *karma*, in order to use up some of the positive or negative *karma* before rebirth. Two rather disparate concepts have thus been neatly brought together. For some, the former will be more important; for others – particularly in popular Hinduism – the latter. At the philosophical level, such differences become more acute with, for example, a school of thought such as Advaita Vedanta accepting a totally monistic view of reality while classical Samkhya advocated plurality as the nature of reality. Originally, there was little to link such opposing schools of thought for classical Samkhya denied the existence of a unifying principle of Brahman. But the moment Brahman is posited – and the Samkhya of the *Gita* does this – ultimate unity is again achieved.

There is much disparity in belief and practice, and many instances when the unity believed to be characteristic of Hinduism is considerably imbalanced. Thus Hindus may describe their religion as *varnasramadharma*, but while *varna* remains important, the four stages of life are more rarely observed. There is a difference too in the religion of the scriptures – the *Sanskritized* element of the religion – and the religious practices of village life. It could be said that the latter, where female divinity is allowed greater expression, do much to balance out the more male-orientated Hinduism of the official texts: theory and practice thus unify well. The concept of a unifying essence of *atman* in Hinduism should serve, theoretically and practically, to overcome excessive differentiation between male and female status in Hinduism. Sadly this is an area where practice does not conform so well to the philosophical idea that male and female are co-existents in perfect balance and unity in the microcosm and macrocosm, in the divine and the human. A film such as the highly acclaimed Indian production of *The Bandit Queen* starkly shows how the imbalance between the sexes has manifested itself, while the status of the male is still of such import that girls are aborted. There are disparities, too, between such concepts as *ahimsa* 'non-violence', and the practice of animal sacrifice, though here, there are many who recognize such imbalance and seek to accord to animals the kind of respect they deserve as manifestations also of one *Ground of all Being*.

The areas of class and caste and ideas of pollution with which they are intimately bound have been shown to overlay so much belief and practice in Hinduism. Theoretically, as was noted at the conclusion of *Part One*, each individual should be free to choose the path to the divine which suits his or her level of consciousness and particular stage of evolution. But caste and location mostly dictates this for an individual. The average Hindu is not so free that he or she would be comfortable to practise an individualized belief beyond the pale of the immediate caste. But then it is the sum total of all past *karma* which places an individual in the kind of life-situation into which he or she is born and which is the best *svadharma* 'personal *dharma*' for that individual. Thus caste in Hindu eyes would be seen, not to prevent evolution or individual freedom in religious belief and practice, but to place the individual in the best position for it to occur.

The way forward

It would be impossible to see unity through all the many examples of diversity and disparity in the broad spectrum of Hinduism, but it is a good starting point for the serious student of Hinduism, to search for the real beneath the apparent, and the concept of unity is one which will provide a good paradigm in many cases. Thus the apparent polytheism of Hindusim, for example, is seen at a deeper level of analysis to be monistic or monotheistic. The existence of Brahman as the substratum of all phenomena is the real unifying principle and the only way to experience such unity within the self is to get rid of the self, to get rid of the process of mind-differentiation between this and that which creates the dualities which obscure the unity of all things as Brahman. Indeed, loss of the egoistic self, which makes such unity possible, could be said to be the common denominator of all Hindu thought.

Individuals are equipped to live life differently, to experience life differently from the next person. They will see only what their personalities will allow them to see, but each individual has a remarkable potential to evolve – even in the confines of the genetic personality. Hinduism recognizes this and seeks to assist the individual on the journey to the fullest potential of one life. A scripture such as the *Gita* exemplifies this well, recognizing that there are very few who are reaching the end of the journey. Hinduism is rich in myth and narrative scripture with many messages both overt and concealed in the words of these scriptures. Individuals have to take from such words what they will and what they can, depending on their level of consciousness: very often the simplest of stories contain the most profound truths and as individual potential is realized the same material can elicit different depths. Hinduism is also rich in symbols; indeed all manifest existence is a symbol of Brahman. Symbols serve to point the mind forward to ideas beyond its immediate conceptions and, generally, Hinduism does this. In the *Introduction* the study of Hinduism was described as a journey and this is what Hinduism is, a journey of the self – the egoistic one – to a point where that ego is lost and the real Self is realized – Brahman.

Notes

1 Fundamental Beliefs

1   See T. W. Organ, *Hinduism: Its Historical Development* (London: Barron's Educational, 1974), p. 15.
2   Part 3, ch. 10:13.

2 Hindu Scriptures

1   R. Dutt, *The Ramayana and the Mahabharata* (New York: Dent, 1978 reprint of 1910 edition), p. 156.

3 *Varnadharma*

1   *Rg Veda* 10:90.
2   D. Killingley et al., *Hindu Ritual and Society* (Newcastle upon Tyne: Grevatt and Grevatt, 1991), p. 5.
3   *Ibid.*, p. 9.

5 Gods and Goddesses

1   See the foreword by A. L. Basham in J. N. Tiwari, *Goddess Cults in Ancient India with Special Reference to the First Seven Centuries AD* (Delhi: Sundeep Prakasham).
2   M. Brand, 'A New Hindu Goddess' *Hemisphere: An Asian Australian Magazine* 26, no. 6 (May/June 1982), p. 382.

6 Worship in the Home and Temple

1   See C. J. Fuller, *The Camphor Flame: Popular Hinduism and Society in India* (India: Viking, 1992), p. 51.
2   *Hinduism Today*, June (1996), vol. 18, no. 6, p. 26.
3   See L. Babb, *The Divine Hierarchy: Popular Hinduism in Central India* (New York: Columbia University Press, 1975), p. 106.

4   Fuller, *The Camphor Flame*, p. 73.
5   *Ibid.*, p. 74.
6   Babb, *The Divine Hierarchy*, pp. 48–9.
7   *Bhagavad Gita* 9:26,27.
8   Fuller, *The Camphor Flame*, p. 70.
9   See A. Mookerji, *Kali: The Feminine Force* (London: Thames and Hudson, 1988), pp. 30ff.

7   Life-cycle Rites in the Hindu Family

1   See Killingley, *Hindu Ritual and Society*, p. 16 and Babb, *The Divine Hierarchy*, p. 79.
2   Babb, *The Divine Hierarchy*, p. 82.
3   See R. Lannoy, *The Speaking Tree* (Oxford: Oxford University Press, 1971), p. 300.
4   See Fuller, *The Camphor Flame* p. 22.
5   See O. Cole and V. P. Kanitkar, *Teach Yourself World Faiths: Hinduism* (London: NTC Publishing Group Hodder and Stoughton, 1995), p. 53.
6   *The Divine Hierarchy*, p. 82.

8   Symbols

1   *Mandukya Upanisad* 1.1.59, translator A. Daniélou, *The Myths and Gods of India* (Rochester USA: Inner Traditions International, 1991 reprint of 1985 edition), p. 39.
2   See also Mookerji, *Kali: The Feminine Force*, pp. 34–5 for a good description of the lotus in tantric symbolism.

9   Food and Dress

1   P. Bahree, *Hinduism* (London: Batsford, 1984), p. 18.
2   Fuller, *The Camphor Flame*, p. 95.
3   *Bhagavad Gita* 17:8.
4   *Ibid.*, verse 9.
5   *Ibid.*, verse 10.
6   B. Beck, 'Colour and Heat in South Indian Ritual', in *Man (N.S.)*, (1969), vol. 4, pp. 553–72.

10   Hindu Festivals

1   Babb, *The Divine Hierarchy*, p. 30.
2   M. Marriott, 'The Feast of Love' in M. Singer (ed.), *Krishna: Myths, Rites and Attitudes* (Chicago: University of Chicago Press, 1968), pp. 210ff.

3   Fuller, *The Camphor Flame*, p. 109.

12   The Indus Valley Civilization

1   R. Thapar, *A History of India, Vol. 1* (London: Penguin, 1966), p. 26.
2   F. Hardy, 'General remarks on the Religious History of India' in F. Hardy, *The World's Religions: The Religions of Asia* (London: Routledge, 1990 reprint of 1988 edition), p. 40.
3   A. L. Basham, *The Wonder That Was India* (London: Sidgwick and Jackson, 1982 reprint of 1967 third revised edition), p. 24.
4   Y. Masih, *The Hindu Religious Thought: 3000 BC–200 AD* (Delhi: Motilal Banarsidass, 1983), p. 2.
5   R. S. Tripathi, *History of Ancient India* (Delhi: Motilal Banarsidass, 1985 reprint of 1942 edition), p. 16.
6   Basham, *The Wonder That Was India*, p. 16.
7   B. and R. Allchin, *The Rise of Civilization in India and Pakistan* (Cambridge: Cambridge University Press, 1982), p. 213.
8   B. B. Lal, 'The Indus Civilization' in A. L. Basham, *A Cultural History of India* (Oxford: Oxford University Press, 1975), p. 14.
9   See M. Eliade, *A History of Religious Ideas Vol. 1: From the Stone Age to the Eleusian Mysteries*, translator W. R. Trask (Chicago: University of Chicago Press, 1978), p. 125.
10   Masih, *The Hindu Religious Thought*, p. 9, for example, is incorrect when he equates the seated posture of the figure on the seals with the 'seated posture of pranayama and dhyana', the traditional yogic posture.
11   See A. Hiltebeitel, 'The Indus Valley "Proto-Siva", Reexamined through Reflections on the Goddess, the Buffalo, and the Symbolism of *vahanas*' *Anthropos* 73 (1978), pp. 769, 770.
12   *Ibid.*, pp. 768–9.
13   *Ibid.*, p. 771.
14   *The Rise of Civilization in India and Pakistan*, p. 214.
15   A. L. Herman, *A Brief Introduction to Hinduism: Religion, Philosophy and Ways of Liberation* (Boulder, Colorado: Westview Press, 1991), pp. 42–3.
16   Hiltebeitel, 'The Indus Valley "Proto-Siva"', pp. 772, 778.
17   *Ibid.*, p. 780.
18   Masih, *The Hindu Religious Thought*, p. 3.
19   Allchin and Allchin, *The Rise of Civilization in India and Pakistan*, p. 207.
20   Basham, *The Wonder That Was India*, p. 22.
21   Tripathi, *History of Ancient India*, p. 16.
22   Allchin and Allchin, *The Rise of Civilization in India and Pakistan*, p. 133.
23   See Mookerji, *Kali: The Feminine Force*, pp. 34–5.
24   See Basham, *The Wonder That Was India*, p. 24.
25   *A Brief Introduction to Hinduism*, p. 47.

26 *Rg Veda* 10:89:7 and 2:20:7.

13 The Vedic period

1 The term *Aryan* really refers to a group of languages but has become so common a term with reference to the invading people that it would be pedantic not to use it in the sense of an ethnic group.

2 N. C. Chaudhuri, *Hinduism* (Oxford: Oxford University Press, 1979), p. 84.

3 J. C. Heesterman, 'Vedism and Brahmanism' in M. Eliade (ed.), *The Encyclopedia of Religion*, vol. 15 (New York: Macmillan, 1987), p. 217.

4 *Ibid.*, p. 224.

5 T. W. Organ, *Hinduism: Its Historical Development* (Woodbury New York: Barron's Educational Series Inc., 1974), p. 64.

6 F. Hardy, 'Vedic Religion' in F. Hardy (ed.), *The World's Religions: The Religions of Asia* (London: Routledge, 1990 reprint of 1988 edition), p. 44.

7 *Rg Veda* 1:1:9 translator W. O' Flaherty, *The Rig Veda* (Harmondsworth Middlesex: Penguin, 1983 reprint of 1981 edition), p. 99.

8 *Ibid.*, 1:1:2–4.

9 Basham, *The Wonder That Was India*, p. 235.

10 R. C. Zaehner, *Hinduism* (Oxford: Oxford University Press, 1984 reprint of 1962 edition), p. 20.

11 *Rg Veda* 8:48:3, translator R. T. H. Griffith, *The Hymns of the Rgveda* (Delhi: Motilal Banarsidass, 1991 reprint of 1973 new, revised edition).

12 *Ibid.*, verse 15.

13 See Heesterman, 'Vedism and Brahmanism', *ER*, vol. 15, pp. 223–4.

14 Organ, *Hinduism: Its Historical Development*, p. 51.

15 *Rg Veda* 8:14:11, translator O' Flaherty, p. 160.

16 Daniélou, *The Myths and Gods of India*, p. 107.

17 *Rg Veda* 7:89:5, translator Griffiths.

18 *Ibid.*, 5:85:8, translator O' Flaherty, pp. 211–12.

19 Organ, *Hinduism: Its Historical Development*, p. 71.

20 *Rg Veda* 2:33:7, translator Griffith.

21 *Ibid.*, 10:90:2,3.

22 *Ibid.*, 3:62:10.

23 However, cf. the *Atharva Veda* 13:1:56.

24 Heesterman, 'Vedism and Brahmanism', *ER*, vol. 15, p. 226.

25 Organ, *Hinduism: Its Historical Development*, p. 63.

26 *The Myths and Gods of India*, p. 67.

27 R. N. Dandekar 'Vedas' in Eliade, *ER*, vol 15, p. 215.

28 *Rg Veda* 1:24:8, translator Griffith.

29 *The Wonder That Was India*, p. 236.

30 For example Herman, *A Brief Introduction to Hinduism*, p. 59.

31   *Rg Veda* 4:23:8–10.
32   Zaehner, *Hinduism* p. 31.
33   *The Wonder That Was India*, p. 247.
34   *Ibid.*, pp 247–8.
35   *Rg Veda*, p. 25.
36   *Rg Veda* 8:10:2, translator Griffith.
37   1:164:46.
38   Cf., however, *Atharva Veda* 10:2:31–33 and 10:8:44.

14   The Vedanta

1   1:3:28, translator S. Radhakrishnan, *The Principal Upanisads* (New Delhi: Indus, 1994 reprint of 1953 edition), p. 162.
2   E. Lott, *Vedantic Approaches to God* (Library of Philosophy and Religion, London: Macmillan, 1980), p. 1.
3   Sri Aurobindo, *The Upanishads: Texts, Translations and Commentaries* (Pondicherry: Sri Aurobindo Ashram Trust, 1986 2nd impression of 1971 edition), p. 1.
4   K. P. Bahadur, *The Wisdom of the Upanishads* (New Delhi: Sterling Publishers Private Ltd., 1989), p. 1.
5   R. N. Dandekar, 'Vedanta' in Eliade, *ER*, vol 15, p. 208.
6   *The Myths and Gods of India*, p. 5. Cf. also A. Shearer and P. Russell, *The Upanishads* (New York: Harper and Row, 1978), p. 11.
7   *The Call of the Upanishads* (Delhi: Motilal Banarsidass, 1990 reprint of 1970 edition), p. 7.
8   W. K. Mahony, 'Upanisads' in Eliade, *ER*, vol. 15, p. 147.
9   Dandekar, 'Vedanta' in Eliade, *ER*, vol. 15, p. 209.
10   J. Mascaró, *The Upanishads* (London: Penguin, 1965), p. 11.
11   P. Deussen, *The Philosophy of the Upanishads* (New Delhi: Oriental Books Reprint Corporation, 1979, 2nd edition of 1906 publication), pp. 10–15.
12   See Mahony, 'Upanisads' in Eliade, *ER*, vol. 15, p. 149.
13   'Vedanta' in Eliade, *ER*, vol. 15, p. 207.
14   *The Call of the Upanishads*, p. 2.
15   *Ibid.*, p. 3.
16   E. Gough, *The Philosophy of the Upanishads: Ancient Indian Metaphysics* (New Delhi: Cosmo, 1979) p. 45.
17   Aurobindo, *The Upanishads*, p. 3.
18   *The Call of the Upanishads*, p. 230.
19   *Svetasvatara Upanisad* 4:4.
20   Strictly speaking there is a difference between monism and *advaita* in that monism is 'one-ism' whereas *advaita* as a non-dual principle is beyond even one.
21   Gough, *The Philosophy of the Upanishads*, p. 38.
22   See J. C. Heesterman, 'Brahman', in Eliade, *ER*, vol. 2, p. 295.

23 4:4:22.

24 4:2:1.

25 *Chandogya Upanisad* 6:1:3, translator Radhakrishnan.

26 *Ibid.*, 6:12:2,3.

27 *Taittiriya Upanisad* 2:1:11.

28 *The Wisdom of the Upanishads*, p. 4.

29 Mahony, 'Upanisads' in Eliade, *ER*, vol. 15, p. 147.

30 See Daniélou, *The Myths and Gods of India*, p. 17 and *Chandogya Upanisad* 7:25.

31 Gough, *The Philosophy of the Upanishads*, p. 36.

32 *Ibid.*, p. 46.

33 *Ibid.*, p. 45.

34 3:20 translator Radhakrishnan, p. 730.

35 Lott, *Vedantic Approaches to God*, p. 7.

36 *Ibid.*, pp. 6–7.

15 Devotional Hinduism

1 M. Biardeau, *Hinduism: The Anthropology of a Civilization* translated by Richard Nice (Delhi: Oxford University Press, 1992 impression of 1989 English translation), p. 91.

2 J. B. Carman, 'Bhakti' in Eliade, *ER*, vol. 2, p. 130.

3 *Ibid.*

4 L. Hess, 'Indian Religious Poetry' in Eliade, *ER*, vol. 11, p. 374.

5 R. Lannoy, *The Speaking Tree: A study of Indian Culture and Society* (New York: Oxford University Press, 1974 edition of 1971 publication), p. 205.

6 See D. Kinsley, *The Sword and the Flute: Dark Visions of the Terrible and the Sublime in Hindu Mythology* (California: University of California Press, 1975), p. 65.

7 F. W. Clothey, 'Tamil Religions' in Eliade, *ER*, vol. 15, p. 262.

8 *The Speaking Tree*, p. 206.

9 18:64–66.

10 S. S. Subramuniyaswami, *Dancing with Siva* (California: USA Himalayan Academy, 1993), p. 25.

11 See D. Kinsley, *Hindu Goddesses: Visions of the Divine Feminine in the Hindu Religious Tradition* (Delhi: Motilal Banarsidass, 1987), pp. 79–80.

12 See M. Singer, 'The Radha-Krishna *Bhajanas* of Madras City' in M. Singer (ed.), *Krishna: Myths, Rites and Attitudes* (Chicago: University of Chicago Press, 1968), p. 129.

13 L. Siegel, *Sacred and Profane Dimensions of Love in Indian Traditions as Exemplified in the* Gitagovinda *of Jayadeva* (Delhi: Oxford University Press, 1990 reprint of 1978 edition), p. 21.

14 See Kinsley, *The Sword and the Flute*, p. 64.

15 See Singer, 'The Radha-Krishna *Bhajanas* of Madras City', p. 132.

16 *Ibid.*
17 Kinsley, *Hindu Goddesses*, p. 82.
18 Cited in A. K. Ramanujan (translator), *Speaking of Siva* (Harmondsworth: Penguin, 1973), p. 125, number 88.
19 F. E. Hardy, 'Krsnaism' in Eliade, *ER*, vol. 8, p. 390.
20 *Bhagavad Gita* 8:14.
21 *The Anthropology of a Civilization*, p. 117.
22 *Ibid.*, p. 113.
23 *Ibid.*
24 *Ibid.*, p. 120.
25 D. N. Lorenzen, 'Saivism' in Eliade, *ER*, vol. 13, p. 9.
26 *Bhagavad Gita* 10:41,42.
27 *Collected Poems and Plays of Rabindranath Tagore* (London: Macmillan, 1983 reprint of 1936 edition), LXXXIII:1, p. 217.

Glossary

A guide to pronunciation of Sanskrit words

Sanskrit has a number of letters representing the English '*s*'. Where the pronunciation of the '*s*' in the Sanskrit is as *sh*, as in English *she*, this will be indicated: where not indicated the pronunciation is an ordinary '*s*' as in English *sat*. Sanskrit also has a number of aspirated letters indicated with an '*h*' following the consonant. When these combinations of letters occur, the reader is advised to separate the two consonants in pronunciation to gain a more accurate sound: thus *artha* 'wealth' is *art* (as in English *art*) plus *ha* (as in English *have*). The particular sound *th* as in English *that* or *theatre* should be avoided. Sanskrit consonants carry the vowel '*a*' with them, which is why translated Sanskrit words have so many '*a*'s in them, like *Mahabharata*. This '*a*' is normally more like the '*u*' in the English word *but*. Where this is not so, diacritical marks are usually added in transliteration to indicate a change of sound. The text of the book does not contain these indicators but the reader will acquire a nearer pronunciation by using a '*u*' sound rather than the long '*a*' as in *father*.

adharma	contrary to what is right; evil. Cf. *dharma*.
Aditi	Vedic goddess, the 'mother' of the gods.
Adityas	Vedic sun deities, offspring of Aditi.
advaita	non-dualism.
Agamas	mystical scriptures pertaining to specific Hindu sects such as Vaisnavaites or Saivites.
Agni	Vedic god of fire.
ahimsa	non-violence.
amma	mother, a compound often used in the names of female goddesses.
amrta	a nectar which was believed to bestow immortality.
ananda	bliss; the bliss of union with Brahman.
Aranyakas	forest writings; mystical Vedic treatises which prefigure much Vedantic thought.

Arjun	one of the sons of Pandu and the main (human) character of the *Bhagavad Gita*.
artha	wealth and social status.
arti	act of worship celebrating light.
Aryans	migrant invaders of India from approximately 1500 BCE.
asat	non-being, that is to say the unreality of the world as opposed to the true Being (*sat*) which is Brahman.
asram	(pronounced *ashram*) place of quiet and solitude, often in a forest, where a Hindu sage lives alone or with his disciples.
asramas	(pronounced *ashramas*) the four stages of life in Hinduism.
asvamedha	(pronounced *ashvamedha*) probably the most prestigious of Vedic sacrificial rites.
Atharva Veda	'Knowledge of Incantations', one of the four *Vedas*.
atman	the presence of Brahman as the deepest essence of the self in all entities; a synonym of Brahman.
aum	the sacred sound and symbol which represents Brahman in its unmanifest and manifest aspects.
avatars	literally 'descents', the incarnations of Visnu and his consort Laksmi.
avidya	ignorance.
Bhagavad Gita	Hindu scripture dated to approximately the first two centuries BCE.
bhajans	hymns in praise of a deity.
bhakta	ardent devotee of a deity who expresses loving-devotion to the divine.
bhakti	ecstatic loving-devotion to the divine.
bhakti marga	the path of devotion.
bindi	mark worn on the centre of the forehead to show that a woman is married.
Brahma	Creator God.
brahmachari	young boy at the first of the four stages of life, the stage of the student.
Brahman	the impersonal Absolute of Hinduism which is the source of all manifest existence and which is present in all things as their deepest essence or *atman*.
Brahmanas	manuals of instruction on the *Vedas*.
Brahmin	a priest and member of the most prestigious of the four classes of Hinduism.
chela	disciple and student of a *guru*.
cit	the Pure Consciousness equated with *moksa* when the egoistic self is lost.
dalit	person outside the class system of Hinduism who was formerly termed an Untouchable.

darsan	(pronounced *darshan*) literally 'view' or 'sight of' referring to audience with a deity.
Darsanas	writings of the six philosophical schools of Hindu religious thought.
deva	male deity; literally 'shining one'.
devi	female deity.
dharma	what is right for the self, the class and caste, society and the universe.
Dharma Sastras	(pronounced *Dharma Shastras*) Law Books forming part of the scriptures of Hinduism.
Divali	Hindu festival.
Durga	Hindu Goddess, one of the energy forms of Siva.
Dussehra	Hindu festival.
dvandva	dualities; pairs of opposites.
dvija	twice-born, referring to those of the three classes of *Brahmins, Ksatriyas* and *Vaisyas* who undergo initiation into the Hindu religion at a sacred ceremony.
Ganesh	Hindu God of Good Fortune.
Ganesh Chaturhi	Hindu festival.
garbagriha	literally 'womb-house', the central part of a temple where the main deity is enshrined.
gauna	the ceremony marking the departure of a bride for the home of her new husband.
gopis	cowherdesses.
gramadevatas	village deities.
grhastha	person at the second of the four stages of life, the stage of the householder.
gunas	the three qualities or strands (like the strands of a rope), *sattva, rajas*, and *tamas*, which constitute all life.
guru	enlightened spiritual teacher.
Hanuman	monkey general who rescued Sita from the demon Ravan in the *Ramayan*, now deified.
havan	an offering of fire in Hindu worship.
Holi	Hindu festival.
Indra	Vedic god of storm and thunder who was also king of the gods.
ista-devata	(pronounced *ishta devata*) chosen deity.
Isvara	(pronounced *Ishvara*) Lord, the term used of God in manifest form.
Itihasas	scriptures which convey historical and mythological sagas and tales.
jati	birth and the caste system.

jivatman	the personality self.
jnana	intuitive knowledge.
jnana marga	the path of knowledge.
jutha	the 'left-overs' of food offered to a deity, the deity having extracted the essence of the food.
kalas	(pronounced *kalash*) brass pot containing water, representative of a goddess.
Kali	Goddess characterized by ferocious appearance.
kama	pleasure, particularly sexual pleasure.
karma	literally 'action' but also the theory of cause and effect i.e. action and reaction.
karma marga	the path of egoless action.
katcha	poor quality, impure food.
kirtan	hymn in praise of a deity.
Krisna	(pronounced Krishna) Hindu deity who is an incarnation of the great God Visnu.
Krisna-Janamastami	Hindu festival.
Ksatriya	(pronounced *Kshatriya*) person belonging to the second of the four Hindu classes of society, traditionally a warrior, ruler or administrator.
Laksman	(pronounced Lakshman) the brother of Ram in the *Ramayan*.
Laksmi	(pronounced Lakshmi) female Goddess of Fortune and consort of Visnu, sometimes called Sri.
linga	phallic symbol associated with the God Siva.
loka	place; realm, as the *deva loka*, the realm of the gods.
Mahabharat	Hindu epic scripture.
Mahadeva	'Great God', one of the names of the deity Siva.
Mahadevi	'Great Goddess', the Mother Goddess of Hinduism.
Mahasivatri	(pronounced *Mahashivatri*) Hindu festival.
mandal	Hindu temple which can also be used for socio-cultural purposes.
mandap/mandva	the canopy under which a wedding ceremony takes place.
mandir	a Hindu temple.
mantra	sacred syllables or sounds which contain in their essence divine cosmic power.
mata	mother, a compound often used in the names of female goddesses.
maya	illusion, particularly the illusion of the transient, impermanent, phenomenal world.
mehndi	long-lasting pattern made with henna dye on the hands of a woman at her wedding and sometimes at festival occasions.
moksa	liberation from the cycle of reincarnation, loss of the egoistic

self, and union with Brahman.

monism	the theory that everything in the cosmos is a unity and is equated with the divine.
monotheism	belief in one personal god or goddess.
murti	the image and representation of a deity in a temple, shrine or in the home.
Namaskar/ Namaste	'I bow to you', the greeting which acknowledges the *atman* in another person.
Navaratri	Hindu festival.
neti neti	literally 'not this, not this', the expression used to denote that Brahman is beyond all dualities and human thought.
nirakara	'without form', referring to Brahman as Unmanifest.
nirguna	'without *gunas*', 'without qualities', referring to Brahman as Unmanifest.
nitya	'obligatory', referring to aspects of religious practice.
panda	a temple priest at a pilgrimage site.
panentheism	the belief that the divine is in all things and unifies all things but is ultimately greater than all things.
pantheism	the belief that the divine is in all things and is equated with the totality of all.
Parvati	Goddess, the consort of the God Siva.
pinda	four balls of rice prepared on the twelfth day after someone has died to symbolize the union of the deceased with his or her forebears.
polytheism	belief in many personal gods and/or goddesses.
prasad	the grace of the deity given to the worshipper in the form of food after worship: see also *jutha*.
puja	honour, respect or worship of a deity.
pujari	temple or shrine priest who performs puja.
pukka	good quality food which is considered ritually pure.
purohit	a family priest or *guru*.
Purusa	(pronounced Purusha), literally 'person': the original, primeval being the sacrifice of which was believed to create from its body the phenomenal world, in particular the four classes. Also a synonym of Brahman and therefore of *atman*.
Radha	a cowherdess who was the favourite of Krisna and an incarnation of the Goddess Laksmi, also a Goddess in her own right.
raja	a tribal chieftain, local ruler or monarch.
rajas	one of the three *gunas* or qualities in existence, associated with the creator God Brahma and representing the active energy in the universe.

rakhi	a band symbolizing protection which is tied round the wrists of males by girls at the festival of *Raksa Bandhan*.
Raksa Bandan	(pronounced *Raksha Bandhan*) Hindu festival.
Ram	An incarnation of the deity Visnu and hero of the epic the Ramayan.
Ramayan	Hindu epic scripture.
Ram Navami	Hindu festival.
Rg Veda	'Royal knowledge', one of the four *Vedas*, the major Aryan scriptures.
rsis	Vedic seers, enlightened men who composed Vedic hymns and *upanisads*.
rta	the Vedic cosmic norm which regulated all existence and to which all had to conform.
sadharana dharma	what is right in terms of the common duties and obligations to one's fellow human beings.
saguna	manifest, referring to manifest aspects of Brahman.
Saivites	(pronounced Shaivites) devotees of the deity Siva.
sakara	'with form', referring to the manifest aspects of Brahman.
sakti	(pronounced *shakti*) the female active energy in the universe.
Sama Veda	'Knowledge of Chants', one of the four *Vedas*.
samsara	reincarnation.
samskaras	life-cycle rites.
sanatana-dharma	what is right for the universe.
sannyasin	person at the last of the four stages of life, the stage of the wandering ascetic.
Santosi Ma	(pronounced Santoshi Ma) a modern Hindu goddess.
saptapadi	the seven steps taken by a couple during their marriage ceremony symbolizing seven different wishes for the future.
sari	traditional dress for women consisting of a piece of material of five or six metres long which is draped around the body.
sat	the Being, Truth and Reality associated with Brahman as opposed to the non-being (*asat*) of the phenomenal world.
Sati	consort of the God Siva, also called Uma.
sati	voluntary burning of a widow on her husband's funeral pyre.
sattva	one of the three *gunas* or qualities in existence, associated with the preserving God Visnu and representing light and spiritual evolution.
Savitr	Vedic solar deity.
Sita	the wife of Ram in the Hindu epic the *Ramayan* and an *avatar* of the Goddess Laksmi.
Siva	(pronounced Shiva) one of the major deities of Hinduism.

smrti	literally 'memory' or 'remembered': a category of sacred scriptures which contains much popular and devotional literature.
Soma	Vedic deity equated also with a potent hallucinogenic drink.
sraddha	(pronouned *shraddha*) ceremonies for the deceased in the twelve days following cremation.
srauta	(pronounced *shrauta*) official sacrificial ritual of the Vedic period.
Sri	(pronounced Shri) the Goddess Laksmi, consort of Visnu.
sruti	pronounced *shruti*) category of sacred scriptures which are 'heard' or cognized by the ancient seers.
Sudra	(pronounced *Shudra*) the fourth of the Hindu four classes, traditionally the servant class.
Surya	Vedic solar deity.
svadharma	what is right for an individual.
tamas	one of the three *gunas* or qualities in existence, associated with the dissolver God Siva and representing the inertia aspect in existence.
Tantras	esoteric, mystical teachings.
tat tvam asi	'That art thou', the equating of the *atman* and every being in total identity with *That*, which is Brahman.
theism	belief in a personal god, goddess, gods or goddesses.
tilak	the mark placed on the forehead of a devotee during ritual worship.
Trimurti	literally 'three-form', the Hindu trinity of three deities, Visnu, Siva and Brahma, representing the three qualities or *gunas* of all existence.
Ugadi	Hindu festival.
Uma	consort of the deity Siva.
upanayama	ceremony of the sacred thread undertaken by the top three classes.
Upangas	literature concerned with ritual and logical thought.
Upanisads	(pronounced *Upanishad*) scriptures occuring at the end of the *Vedas* characterized by mystical and philosophical speculation on the nature of the self and ultimate Reality.
Upavedas	additions to the Vedic scriptures.
Usas	(pronounced Ushas) Vedic goddess of dawn.
Vaisnavites	(pronounced Vaishnavites) devotees of the deity Visnu.
Vaisya	(pronounced *Vaishya*) person belonging to the third of the four Hindu classes of society, traditionally an artisan or skilled labourer.
vanaprastha	person at the third of the four stages of life, the stage of the forest dweller.
varna	literally 'colour', the word for the four-class system in Hinduism.

varnasrama-dharma	what is right for class and stage of life.
Varuna	Vedic deity of cosmic order.
Veda	knowledge.
Vedangas	rules on ritual, astronomy, morals, grammar and phonetics.
Vedas	the four Vedic scriptures of *Rg, Sama, Yajur* and *Atharva*.
vidya	knowledge.
Visnu	(pronounced Vishnu) one of the major deities of Hinduism.
yajna	sacrificial ritual.
Yajur Veda	'Knowledge of Sacrificial Ritual', one of the four *Vedas*.
Yama	ruler of the realm of the dead the 'Land of the Fathers': he was the first man to die and therefore the welcomer of others to his realm.
yatra	pilgrimage.
yoga	discipline or 'yoking' of the senses and the ego.

Select Bibliography

General reference works

An excellent source for all aspects of Hinduism is the 16-volume *Encyclopedia of Religion* edited by Mircea Eliade, published in 1987, New York, Macmillan. Under the entry of 'Hinduism' in the general index of volume 16 is a comprehensive list of the articles to be found in the *Encyclopedia*. Each article is accompanied by a bibliography relating to the specific topic. An overview of Hinduism is to be found in volume 6, pp. 336–60. Articles specifically relevant to *Part One: The Hindu Way of Life* and to *Part Two: History and Tradition* will be included in the categories below with a reference to the *Encyclopedia* as *ER* together with the appropriate volume and pages.

Primary sources

Aurobindo, Sri. 1986 2nd. impression of 1971 edition: *The Upanishads: Texts, Translations and Commentaries*. Pondicherry: Sri Aurobindo Ashram Trust.

Dutt, R. 1978 reprint of 1910 edition: *The Ramayana and the Mahabharata*. New York: Dent.

Edgerton, F. 1994; (first published 1944): *The Bhagavad Gita*. Delhi: Motilal Banarsidass.

Embree, A. T. (ed.), 1988: *Sources of Indian Tradition: Volume 1: From the Beginning to 1800*. New York: Columbia University Press.

Embree, A. T. (ed.), 1972 (first published 1966): *The Hindu Tradition: Readings in Oriental Thought*. New York: Vintage.

Griffith, R. T. H. 1991 reprint of 1973 revised edition: *The Hymns of the Rgveda*. Delhi: Motilal Banarsidass.

Johnson, W. J. 1994: *The Bhagavad Gita*. Oxford: Oxford University Press.

Mascaró, J. 1962: *The Bhagavad Gita*. Harmondsworth, Middlesex: Penguin.

Mascaró, J. 1965: *The Upanishads*. London: Penguin.

O'Flaherty, W. D. 1975: *Hindu Myths*. Harmondsworth, Middlesex: Penguin.

O'Flaherty, W.D. 1988: *Textual Sources for the Study of Hinduism*. Manchester: Manchester University Press.

O'Flaherty, W. 1983 reprint of 1988 edition: *The Rig Veda*: Harmondsworth, Middlesex: Penguin.

Olivelle, P. 1996: *Upanisads*. Oxford: Oxford University Press.

Parrinder, G. 1996 (first published 1974): *The Bhagavad Gita: A Verse Translation*. Oxford: One World.

Radhakrishnan, S. 1994 reprint of 1953 edition: *The Principal Upanisads*. New Delhi: Indus.

Radhakrishnan, S. and Moore, C. A. (eds.), 1989 reprint of 1957 edition: *A Sourcebook in Indian Philosophy*. Princeton, New Jersey: Princeton University Press.

Ramanujan, A. K. (translator) 1973: *Speaking of Siva*. Harmondsworth: Penguin.

Shearer, A. and Russell, P. 1978: *The Upanishads*. New York: Harper and Row.

Swami, S. P. and Yeats, W.B. 1985 reprint of 1937 edition: *The Ten Principal Upanishads*. London: Faber and Faber.

Wilkins, W. J. 1992 impression of 1975 edition: *Hindu Mythology: Vedic and Puranic*. Calcutta: Rupa and Company.

Zaehner, R. C. 1982 reprint of 1966 edition: *Hindu Scriptures*. London: Dent.

Zaehner, R. C. 1973: first published 1969: *The Bhagavad-Gita*. Oxford: Oxford University Press.

Secondary sources

Part One: The Hindu Way of Life

Altekar, A. S. 1995 reprint of 1959 edition: *The Position of Women in Hindu Civilization*. Delhi: Motilal Banarsidass.

Babb, L. 1975: *The Divine Hierarchy: Popular Hinduism in Central Asia*. New York: Columbia University Press.

Baker, S. 1990: *Caste: At Home in Hindu India*. London: Jonathan Cape.

Barber, R. 1991: *Pilgrimages*. Woodbridge, Suffolk: The Boydell Press.

Beck, B. 1969: Colour and Heat in South Indian Ritual. *Man (N.S.)* 4.

Bhardwaj, S. M. 1973: *Hindu Places of Pilgrimage in India: A Study in Cultural Geography*. California: University of California Press.

Biardeau, M. 1992 impression of 1989 English translation: *Hinduism: The Anthropology of a Civilization*, translated by Richard Nice. Delhi: Oxford University Press.

Brand, M. 1992: A New Hindu Goddess, *Hemisphere: An Asian Australian Magazine* 26,6.

Cole, O. and Kanitkar, V. P. 1995: *Teach Yourself World Faiths: Hinduism*. London: NTC Publishing Group Hodder and Stoughton.

Cole, W. O. 1984: *Six Religions in the Twentieth Century*. Amersham, Bucks: Hulton.

Coward, H. G., Lipner, J. J. and Young, K. K. 1989: *Hindu Ethics: Purity, Abortion, and Euthanasia*. Delhi: Sri Satguru Publications.

Daniélou, A. 1991 reprint of 1985 edition: *The Myths and Gods of India*. Rochester USA: Inner Traditions International.

Dumont, L. 1980: (first published in French 1966): *Homo Hierarchicus: The Caste System and Its Implications*. Chicago: University of Chicago Press.

Fuller, C. J. 1992: *The Camphor Flame: Popular Hinduism and Society in India*. India: Viking.

Jackson, R. and Killingley, D. 1988: *World Religions in Education: Approaches to Hinduism*. London: John Murray.

Killingley, D. et al. 1991: *Hindu Ritual and Society*. Newcastle upon Tyne: Grevatt and Grevatt.

Kinsley, D. R. 1993: (first published 1982): *Hinduism: A Cultural Perspective*. New Jersey: Prentice Hall.

Lannoy, R. 1971: *The Speaking Tree*. Oxford: Oxford University Press.

Mackenzie, D. A. 1993: *Myths and Legends: India*. London: Studio Editions.

Mookerji, A. 1988: *Kali: The Feminine Force*. London: Thames and Hudson.

Mukerji, B. 1988: *The Hindu Tradition: An Introduction to Hinduism and to Its Sacred Tradition*. New York: Amity House.

Mukherji, P. 1988: *Beyond the Four Varnas: The Untouchables in India*. Delhi: Motilal Banarsidass.

Narayan, R. K. 1989 reprint of 1987 edition: *The Ramayana*. Delhi: Vision Books.

Pandey, R. 1994 reprint of 1969 edition: *Hindu Samskaras*: Socio-Religious Study of the Hindu Sacraments. Delhi: Motilal Banarsidass.

Subramuniyaswami, S. S. 1993: *Dancing with Siva*. California: Himalayan Academy USA.

Part Two: History and Tradition

Allchin, B. and Allchin, R. 1982: *The Rise of Civilization in India and Pakistan*. Cambridge: Cambridge University Press.

Bahadur, K. P. 1989: *The Wisdom of the Upanishads*. New Delhi: Sterling Publishers Private Limited.

Carmen, J. B. 1987: Bhakti. In *ER*, 2, 130–34.

Dandekar, R. N. 1987: Vedanta. In *ER*, 15, 207–14.

Dandekar, R. N. 1987: Vedas. In *ER*, 15, 214–17.

Deussen, P. 1979 2nd. edition of 1906 publication: *The Philosophy of the Upanishads*. New Delhi: Oriental Books Reprint Corporation.

Gough, E. 1979: *The Philosophy of the Upanishads: Ancient Indian Metaphysics*. New Delhi: Cosmo.

Hardy, F. E. 1987: Krisnaism. In *ER*, 8, 387–92.

Hardy, F. 1990 reprint of 1988 edition:The classical religions of India. In F. Hardy (ed.), *The World's Religions: The Religions of Asia*. London: Routledge, 37–71.

Heesterman, J. C. 1987: Brahman. In *ER* 2, 294–96.

Heesterman, J. C. 1987: Vedism and Brahmanism. In *ER* 15, 217–42.

Herman, A. L. 1991: *A Brief Introduction to Hinduism: Religion, Philosophy and Ways of Liberation*. Boulder, Colorado: Westview Press.

Hess, L. 1987: Indian Religious Poetry. In *ER*, 11, 374–78.

Hiltebeitel, A. 1978: The Indus Valley "Proto-Siva" reexamined through reflections on the goddess, the buffalo, and the symbolism of *vahanas*, *Anthropos* 73, 767–97.

Kinsley, D. 1975: *The Sword and the Flute: Dark Visions of the Terrible and the Sublime in Hindu Mythology*. California: University of California Press.

Kinsley, D. 1987: *Hindu Goddesses: Visions of the Divine Feminine in the Hindu Religious Tradition*. Delhi: Motilal Banarsidass.

Lal, B. B. 1975: The Indus civilization. In Basham, A.L. (ed.), *A Cultural History of India*. Oxford: Oxford University Press.

Lorenzen, D. N. 1987: Saivism. In *ER*, 13, 6–11.

Lott, E. 1980: *Vedantic Approaches to God*. Library of Philosophy and Religion, London: Macmillan.

Mahony, W. K. 1987: Upanisads. In *ER*, 15, 147–52.

Masih, Y. 1983: *The Hindu Religious Thought 3000 BC–200 AD*. Delhi: Motilal Banarsidass.

Mehta, R. 1990 reprint of 1970 edition: *The Call of the Upanishads*. Delhi: Motilal Banarsidass.

Organ, T. W. 1974: *Hinduism: Its Historical Development*. London: Barron's Educational.

Siegel, L. 1990 reprint of 1978 edition: *Sacred and Profane Dimensions of Love in Indian Traditions as Exemplified in the* Gitagovinda *of Jayadeva*. Delhi: Oxford University Press.

Singer, M. 1968: The Radha-Krishna *bhajanas* of Madras city. In M. Singer (ed.), *Krishna: Myths, Rites and Attitudes*. Chicago: University of Chicago Press.

Thapar, R. 1996: *A History of India Vol 1*. London: Penguin.

Tripathi, R. S. 1985 reprint of 1942 edition: *History of Ancient India*. Delhi: Motilal Banarsidass.

1983 reprint of 1936 edition: *Collected Poems and Plays of Rabindranath Tagore*. London: Macmillan.

General sources

Bailey, G. M. and Watson, I. K. 1992: *Bhakti Studies*. Delhi: Sterling Publishers Private Limited.

Basham, A. L. 1975: *A Cultural History of India*. Delhi: Oxford University Press.

Basham, A. L. 1982 reprint of 1967 third, revised edition: *The Wonder That Was India*. London: Sidgwick and Jackson.

Bhattacharya, B. 1988: *The World of Tantra*. Delhi: Munshiram Manoharlal Publishers Private Limited.

Buck, W. 1973: *Mahabharata*. New York: Mentor.

Buck, W. 1978: *Ramayana*. New York: Mentor.

Chakravarti, M. 1986: *The Concept of Rudra-Siva through the Ages*. Motilal Banarsidass.

Chaudhuri, N.C. 1979: *Hinduism*. Oxford: Oxford University Press.

Cross, S. 1994: *The Elements of Hinduism*. Shaftesbury, Dorset: Element.

Dowson, J. 1991 impresssion of 1982 edition: *A Classical Dictionary of Hindu Mythology and Religion: Geography, History and Literature*. Calcutta: Rupa and Company.

Eastman, R. 1993 reprint of 1975 edition: *The Ways of Religion: An Introduction to the Major Traditions*. Oxford: Oxford University Press, pp. 7–60.

Hopkins, T. J. 1971: *The Religious Life of Man: The Hindu Religious Tradition*. California: Wadsworth Publishing Company.

Koller, J. M. 1982: *The Indian Way*. New York: Macmillan.

Kosambi, D. D. 1991 reprint: *The Culture and Civilization of Ancient India in Historical Outline*. Delhi: Vikas Publishing House Private Limited.

Ling, T. 1990 reprint of 1968 edition: *A History of Religion East and West*. London: Macmillan.

Madan, T. N. 1987: *Non-Renunciation: Themes and Interpretations of Hindu Culture*. Delhi: Oxford University Press.

Marriott, M. 1968: The Feast of Love. In M. Singer (ed.), *Krishna: Myths Rites and Attitudes*. Chicago: University of Chicago Press, 200–212.

Narayan, R. K. 1991 reprint of 1987 edition: (first published 1964): *Gods, Demons, and Others*. Delhi: Vision Books.

Nigosian, S. A. 1994: *World Faiths*. New York: St. Martin's Press.

O'Flaherty, W. D. 1981: (first published 1973): *Siva: The Erotic Ascetic*. Oxford: Oxford University Press.

Smart, N. 1971; (first published 1969): *The Religious Experience of Mankind*. Glasgow: Collins.

Smith, H. 1991: *The World's Religions*. San Fransisco: Harper.

Vyas, R.N. 1983: *Melody of Bhakti and Enlightenment*. Delhi: Cosmo Publications.

Zaehner, R. C. 1984 reprint of 1962 edition: *Hinduism*. Oxford: Oxford University Press.

Articles in edited sources

Basham, A. L. 1991 reprint of 1959 edition: Hinduism. In Zaehner, R. C. *Hutchinson Encyclopedia of Living Faiths*. Glasgow: Hutchinson, pp. 217–54.

Hammer, R. 1982: The Eternal Teaching: Hinduism. In *The World's Religions*, Tring: Lion pp. 170–196.

Weightman, S. 1988 reprint of 1988 edition: Hinduism. In Hinnells, J. R. (ed.), *A Handbook of Living Religions*. Harmondsworth, Middlesex: Penguin, pp. 191–236.

Index